OUR GOD
HAS NO
FAVOURITES

OUR GOD HAS NO FAVOURITES

A Liberation Theology of the Eucharist

Anne Primavesi
and
Jennifer Henderson

Burns & Oates
Tunbridge Wells, England

Resource Publications, Inc.
San Jose, California

First published in Great Britain 1989
Burns & Oates Ltd,
Wellwood, North Farm Road,
Tunbridge Wells, Kent TN2 3DR

First published in the United States of America by
Resource Publications, Inc.
160 E. Virginia Street #290
San Jose, California CA 95112.

Front cover calligraphy by Peter Thornton

As this book has been published simultaneously in the United
States of America and Great Britain, English spelling has been
used within the text.

Library of Congress Cataloguing in Publication Data Available

5 4 3 2 1

93 92 91 90 89

ISBN (UK) 0 86012 170 4
ISBN (USA) # 0–89390–165 2

Typeset by Scribe Design, Gillingham, Kent
Printed and bound in Great Britain by
Biddles Ltd, Guildford and King's Lynn

For Mark and Desmond

Foreword

by JAMES D. G. DUNN

THIS BOOK IS a cry from the heart. It is a cry the churches and the guardians of church tradition need to hear. For it calls us to face squarely the hard fact that several of our most sacred and cherished practices have departed in marked degree from the practices of Jesus himself and his apostles. So much so as to *betray* principles and attitudes which were clearly fundamental to the religious practice they sought to encourage.

Of course practices have developed and changed vastly over the centuries; as we would expect. A church which did not change would die. Such is the law of both natural and spiritual development. But the question is whether the changed and developed practices remain true to the spirit and principles which came to expression in these practices in the first place. The blunt charge levelled in this book is that in key areas of church life we have been unfaithful stewards.

The lament justifiably focuses on the Eucharist. What *are* we to say when we compare the practice of Jesus and his first disciples with current practice? On the one hand, a table fellowship which welcomed sinners (e.g. Mark 2:15–17; Matt. 11:19). Again, a resolute refusal to let differences prevent the enjoyment of table-communion– even major differences regarding what Christianity was (Rom. 14). 'Welcome one another as Christ has welcomed you, for the glory of God' (Rom. 15:7). On the other hand, the equally resolute refusal of current practice to welcome fellow Christians to the shared bread and cup. Once again 'the righteous' refuse communion to 'the sinners'! Once again 'Jews' refuse to eat with 'Gentiles'! What can we be thinking of? What must our Lord and the Apostles to (us) gentiles think of us?

It is really no longer good enough to say that the sharing of each other's table must await a genuine unity. The shared table is at the heart of Jesus' ministry and Paul's gospel. It is the only mark of our mutual acceptance which really counts. Without it we have *not* accepted each other, whatever our professions to the contrary. 'We' are still 'the righteous' and 'they' are still 'the sinners', those other so-called Christians!

And then there is the matter of the meal. It is no accident that the Eucharist began in the context of a meal–indeed *as* a meal. The bread and the wine bring into focus the fellowship and communion of the meal table. The bread at the beginning, the cup 'after supper'. Have we not lost something here too? A horizontal dimension, a festive occasion. (Jesus, you will recall, was described as 'a glutton and a drunkard'–Matt. 11:19). Rich as our eucharistic practice now is, and richly resonant with echoes of centuries past, beside the practice of Jesus and the first Christians it is still nevertheless impoverished. As full of symbolism as the wafer and the sip of wine are, the bread and cup within the family meal and the fellowship meal of the church in the home are so much richer in symbolism–and in the reality of the shared meal which mattered so much to Jesus and Paul.

But, of course, if we pursue that line of thought then we threaten the 'great gulf fixed' between clergy and laity. After all, it has been control of the sacred food which has been the secret of priestly power and privilege. How ironic that the bread and wine, which Jesus used in order to break down such barriers, have been transformed into the most fundamental barrier now remaining within the people of God. For a Christian student of the New Testament it really is astonishing and distressing that these distinctions between priest and people should have re-emerged in Christianity and have become so entrenched within the catholic tradition. For if the New Testament writers are agreed on anything it is that the distinction within God's people between some who are priests and some who are not has been left behind. Under Christ either all share a common priesthood, or Christ is literally the only priest. *Tertium non datur*.

And let us not forget that the cry of pain in this book is a cry of two women. It simply will not be good enough to dismiss or discount this cry either, as merely pandering to twentieth-century prejudices. As the authors point out, it was Jesus who broke with religious etiquette and taboos of his day by accepting the 'ministry' of women to him. And it was Paul who speaks of Junia as 'eminent among the apostles' (Rom. 16:7: no Greek would have read it as 'Junias', masculine). Any student of the New Testament knows that the circle of apostles was larger than the twelve–including, for a start, James the brother of Jesus, and Paul. A leading figure among these, Paul reminds us, was a woman and (probably) a wife (of Andronicus). How unbalanced is our reading of scripture which has allowed us to ignore such scriptures so completely and for so long.

It would not be difficult to prolong the argument. But I have said enough to indicate that the authors' cry from the heart is echoed by at least one other. As the old-time writers used to say, I invite you, dear reader, carefully to read, mark and reflect on what follows. Maybe when enough people begin to cry out together someone will hear. 'Our God has *no* favourites'.

University of Durham
February 1989

ix

CONTENTS

Introduction

EVERY TIME WE meet to break bread together we give thanks for the indiscriminate love of God for us all. We eat and drink in the name of the Son whose life was the gift of the Father's love to the world. This book witnesses to our experience of this love through the power of the Spirit.

The title: *Our God has no Favourites*, picks up themes in the Jewish Scriptures, in Acts, in Paul, in James (Deut. 10:17; Acts 10:16; Rom. 2:11; James 2:1). Stressing the impartiality of God's love for the world reminds us of the partial nature of our own love. We can never settle for that partiality if we are to witness to divine love. Above all, we cannot settle for it at the moment of communal witness we call Eucharist. When a Christian community breaks bread and shares the cup together in union with the Son and the Spirit, it 'eucharistizes,' that is, it gives thanks for God's great love for the whole world. This communal witness is essential today in a world under threat from every kind of division, including ultimate fragmentation into nuclear dust.

But when we added the sub-title, 'A Liberation Theology of the Eucharist' an objection was raised. For this particular brand of theology states categorically that God *does* have favourites: the poor. So how could we talk about the indiscriminate love of God for us all, and yet claim to be 'doing' liberation theology?

Our contention is that this claim can be made because what we have to say springs from the experience of those furthest from the centres of power in the Church, the laity: because we want to make a fresh attempt at freeing the Churches *from* something and *for* something; from the scandal of discriminatory eucharistic practices and for the freedom to love one another as Christ loved us–without discrimination. We want also to meet in some way the need for a contemporary theology of the Holy Spirit felt by the liberation theologians themselves. It is the truth which sets us free, that which is taught by the Spirit of truth and promised by Jesus to all disciples.

As the book progressed and various friends helped with their comments on the draft chapters, it became clear that this was not the usual European perception of liberation theology. Attempts were made here and there, notably in Chapter 3, to clarify the term 'poor'. To describe the specific nature of third-world liberation adequately would require another book. Nevertheless the internal debate was valuable, as it reinforced our claim to the sub-title by forcing us to express our view of what makes a theology liberative. We had to make an explicit connection between what is done in the Third World and what we are trying to do.

As it is usually read in North Atlantic countries, liberation theology is associated with the struggle for economic and social justice. A glance at the most famous titles and authors classified under this heading in libraries or bookshops confirms this. Yet behind such theology lies a process familiar enough to everyone. This is the living interaction between the Word of God evidenced in the scriptures and the human experience of those who read or hear that Word.

What gives this theology its peculiar power is the human experience in which the Word of God is received. It is hard to improve on Moltmann's description of this: 'Reading the Bible with the eyes of the poor is a different thing from reading it with the eyes of the man with a full belly. If it is read in the light of the experiences and hopes

2

of the oppressed, the Bible's revolutionary themes—promise, Exodus, resurrection and Spirit—come alive![1]

This kind of reading belongs primarily to the economically deprived regions of the world. However, as Moltmann points out, liberation from oppression is an 'open concept', exemplified most clearly in the material deprivation of the poor, but which embraces all the different dimensions of suffering. It runs from the abolition of economic exploitation and the cultural elimination of racialism down to faith's experience of liberation from the compulsion of sin. In all instances it tries to grapple with structures and systems which dehumanize. Therefore in the Third World the provision of proper living standards, education and self-organization is argued for by the theologians, as these counteract the direct effects of mass economic and political deprivation.

As these liberative processes are worked through, the interaction of the life of the poor and the Word of God acts as catalyst for transforming the powerless into agents of their own and others' freedom. There are certain moments when the catalytic process becomes evident. One such is the moment when the poor realize that, however devalued they are in the eyes of the society which exploits them, they are of infinite value in the eyes of God. The New Zealand poet and philosopher James Baxter, who left the comfort of his city home to live with a Maori community, describes this moment. He uses the native words, *Te Ariki*, for Christ the Lord:

> The example of Te Ariki is cheering. He did not despair of his friends, faulty as they were. He thought them worth dying for. And since Te Ariki is God himself, none of us need ever feel that God despairs of man.
>
> I think my friends are worth dying for. It is rather myself I might despair of, since I know my own impenetrable darkness and weakness. But in that matter I am obliged to accept the verdict of Te Ariki, who thought otherwise of us

all, and continue on whatever road he opens in front of me, or stand still if he shows me no road.[2]

Another liberative breakthrough comes with the realization that the structures we live with are not the will of God, but are man-made—and therefore they can be dismantled by men. 'It ain't necessarily so' is the first stage on the road to changing how it is.

Closely bound up with this is the moment when the cry for freedom is recognized as a cry for justice, the justice of the Kingdom of God. The 'good news' of this Kingdom is liberation from slavery, hunger, thirst and prison. The unequal distribution of the world's resources actively prevents the majority of those who hunger and thirst being filled. Correcting this imbalance is an act of justice, part of the coming of the Kingdom. This concern for visible justice and all it involves for the Church's self-image is summed up in Dom Helder Camara's famous cry from the heart: 'When I give food to the poor, I am called a saint! But when I ask why the poor have no food, I am called a communist!' The commitment to justice is clear in a Jesuit policy document which declares: 'The way to faith and the way to justice are inseparable ways.'

These complex processes, together with their visible results in social and political reforms, have by and large been written up not by the oppressed themselves, but by an educated minority of theologians. One of the most influential, Jon Sobrino, described what happens to them. The poor, he says, teach us who God is, who Christ is, what sin is. They are 'the conscience of the Church'. The title of one of his books speaks for itself: *The True Church and The Poor*. The poor are seen to have an educational role within the Church.

Theologies like his take account of global economic and political structures as they impinge on those furthest from the centres of power. They analyze the relationships between civil rights and religion: between liberation and oppression; between language and domination; between alternative world visions. The books which result are highly sophisticated philosophical and theological exercises which use the language and concepts of European education to interpret the experience of the uneducated third-world majority populations.

In doing this the theologians impose a particular grid of understanding on what they see and hear about them. How many peasants in Uruguay, El Salvador or Brazil have read Hegel, Marx or Moltmann?

Since most of the third-world theologians are clerics, they must and do take account of the authority structures of their own churches in their analyses of oppressive situations. The clerical authorities in turn monitor the orthodoxy of these writings. This is true for Protestant as well as Roman Catholic theologians.[3]

In practice, then, a system of controls operates on how the primary experience of the uneducated is interpreted. The first lies in the theological analysis itself. The next, that of Church censorship, considers itself final arbiter of what is correct in the interpretation.

This type of liberation theology gives rise to such protests as the one against our sub-title. How can it be authentic if it does not start with 'the option for the poor' enshrined in the declarations of the Latin American Bishops' Conference at Puebla in 1979, and in the Conclusions of the previous one at Medellín in 1968? This option is canonized in such figures as Archbishops Romero and Camara, and is taken for granted by theologians such as Gustavo Gutiérrez, Juan Luis Segundo, José Míguez Bonino and Leonardo and Clodovis Boff. They all teach that God chooses to be found with those who are most deprived materially.

This appears to force liberation theologians in the First World to search for those within that world most economically deprived. This possibility has been taken up in England by such theologians as John Vincent of the Urban

Theology Unit in Sheffield and by all who devote themselves to the 'Faith in the City' programmes. There are similar ventures among immigrant workers in Europe and among blacks in America.

Yet the third-world theologians themselves insist on the relevance of their theology for the *whole* world, not least because it exposes the intricate web of relationships between poverty and affluence, between power and powerlessness, between the management of the global economy and the survival of our common humanity.

But there is a more profound reason still why it is a universal Christian theology. The perspective of poverty and powerlessness reveals the deepest truth about God in Christ. James Baxter writes:

> The slaves lay down to sleep on a straw mattress,
> And most of it made sense. As if God had opened
> A crack in the rock of the world to let some daylight in
> Saying, 'Be poor like Me'.[4]

The compelling aspect of God's poverty mysteriously revealed in Christ is the emptying of himself in death for all, 'while we were yet sinners'. In Baxter's phrase, He thought us all worth dying for, faulty as we are. In Jesus' life, his openness and availability to sinners in their poverty meant he was counted among them, and his death completed the circle of his table companionship with 'evildoers'. To be poor then was not a sign of moral worth any more than it is today. To become poor was not to become good. On the contrary, 'the evils of poverty' was not just an empty phrase: In Jesus's lifetime they included those occupations of the poor which automatically made them 'accursed'.

Seen from the perspective of the poor, then, Jesus's life and teaching has that revolutionary character referred to by Moltmann. It literally turns things upside down. The poor are now the rich, for they live with open and empty

6

hands which God can fill with the joy of companionship. The rich are truly poor, for they live with tightly clenched hands which too easily turn into fists shaken at the Cross. Those who live with open hands belong to the Kingdom. Through the power of the Spirit they remember the death and resurrection of Jesus and the openness of his self-giving whenever bread is broken and wine shared among them.

In the Church today, this revolutionary perspective determines whether or not a theology can be called liberative. The option for the poor is the choice of a particular starting point, that of the powerless. This initial choice determines the emphasis on the worth of the individual devalued by oppressive structures, and on the interaction between the Word of God and human experience. This is true wherever liberation theology is done.

There are differences however, when it is done in North Atlantic countries. It is not necessarily done by clerics, but often by an educated laity. This is the case in the theologies of sexism, racism and ecology being worked out at this time. The clerical interface between the experience of oppression and its expression is done away with. Those oppressed by structures speak for themselves.

This means that a different interpretative grid from the clerical/hierarchical one operates. Therefore such liberation theologians feel free to address themselves explicitly to oppression within the churches as well as outside them. Those who analyze the situation are those who suffer most from it.

A liberation theology of the Eucharist in the First World is concerned with the way in which, in our modern Western tradition, 'the structures of the Church have internalized the class structure of society', as Bonino says.[5] He points out that this necessarily brings into the Church tyrannical forms of exercise of authority. They are derived from sociological patterns of domination and

7

incorporate a class structure into Church hierarchies. (It is a matter of historical record that church order as we know it, including vestments and divisions into dioceses, is based on the Civil Service of the Roman Empire.[6]) Therefore, official ecumenical moves towards full communion are seen almost as a process of diplomatic manoeuvrings, with positions to be negotiated and defended, rather than as a response to the common worthiness and common neediness of all Christians. The laity in turn see their upholding of discriminatory practices at the altar as a matter of loyalty to structures, which repay that loyalty with assurance of security and certainty through a particular 'divine right'.

This is particularly true at this time of stalemate in official negotiations. These were given a 'top-dressing' of optimism in England in September 1987, when more than three hundred representatives from thirty-three Christian denominations met at Swanwick, Derbyshire, to plot a course for Christian unity. But the statements made there about commitment were rendered infertile by ominous warnings about the counter-productivity of ordaining women. The delicate moves on the ecumenical chessboard were back at stalemate once a female pawn moved into the bishop's position.

But the real meaning of ecumenism comes from the word *oikumene* (all the inhabited world). Therefore a liberation theology of the Eucharist describes, in Bonino's words, 'the struggle for the creation of a new *oikumene* in justice to replace the Western modern *oikumene* which is a structure of domination.'[7]

The vision of this new *oikumene* and the power to bring it into being come to the laity in the interaction between the Word of God and their own experience of the modern Western *oikumene*. A world-wide vision of the Eucharist is an awareness of the communion between our common poverty and God's plenty made plain in the sharing of bread. A liberative vision sees and questions the relationship between the 'management' of our unjust eucharistic practices and the survival of our common humanity.

This expansive view of ecumenism brings us back to our main title. Our God has no favourites within all the inhabited world. This statement is given power by the fact that it is made from the perspective of those who can claim no favours within the Church, and who are in no position to grant any. We are the poor with empty open hands. If the gift of the Eucharist is the one supreme gift of life for the world, the laity are not able to give it to those dying of hunger, whether this is called sin or need. But they can cry to the Father for justice, and ask with Dom Helder Camara *why* they and their brothers and sisters are not filled.

The role of the poor within the Third World is an exemplary one. Being on the 'passive' end of the structures of injustice and discrimination in the human community, they are better placed to discern their presence. In the church, the laity have the experience of some sitting in the pews while others go up for Holy Communion; of climbing over one's friends while on the way to receiving alone; of being exhorted to either course of conduct on the grounds of loyalty to one's denomination. This builds up in some to a feeling of oppression and injustice which finds voice in this book. It is not explicitly felt by many who have had their sensibilities dulled by centuries of denigrating their fellow Christians, and is not directly experienced by those who stand at the altar.

Nevertheless, the church authorities themselves feel oppressed by the necessity of either rejecting or upholding the anathemas hurled at one another in the past—and in the present. They feel oppressed by the care of souls in their charge, by their accountability before God and the world for the power to 'bind and loose' (whatever interpretation this may bear). One Catholic university chaplain in England recently resigned his post because of the impossible tensions created for him by rigid rules forbidding him to share communion with students from other Churches.[8]

It does not help that there is a muddled recognition of the suffering involved. Those who do question discriminatory separation at the altar are told that we must 'feel the pain of separation'. Why? Because God wants us to? This is the unspoken and heretical justification lying behind the injunction. A more rational argument would be that pain is a warning symptom in a healthy body, and calls for remedies. It is not a state to be tolerated or maintained. Here again the liberative realization that the rules which constrict our lives and vision are man-made, and the pain self-inflicted, urges us to change. We must learn to act on our own initiatives, disregard institutionalized discrimination and respond instead to Jesus' example and command. He shared without partiality: 'The bread which I shall give for the life of the world is my flesh' (John 6:51). He commanded us to show none when we find ourselves with another community: 'Whenever you enter a town and they receive you, eat what is set before you' (Luke 10:8).

No human community can persist in history without institutionalizing itself, and the New Testament community was no exception. But with this process, as Bonino points out, came the 'institutionalization into the life of the Church of unjust forms of domination, discrimination and privilege, based on race, sex or class. These tend to become sacralized (supposedly God-given) and are then claimed to be normative.'[9]

But the norms of the Kingdom of God, rediscovered in prayerful dialogue between the Word of God and our human experience, keep church norms in perspective. They relativize them and make it possible to alter them where required. Jesus did not come that we might feel the pain of separation, but that we might have abundant life. He did not come to dominate but to serve. He did not break the bruised reed with the heavy hand of authority,

10

or extinguish the smouldering wick of hope in those who came to him to be made clean and upright again. Rather, through the power of the Spirit he proclaimed justice to the Gentiles, those outside his own faith community (cf. Matt. 12:18f).

Through the power of the same Spirit we too can discern and change crippling structures in the Church which 'internalize the class structures of society'. Those who go hungry at our Eucharists are in effect treated as second-class citizens, on the basis that they do not share the hereditary rights of baptism or ministry: the educational qualifications of proper instruction; the social privileges of acceptable codes of behaviour. The scandal of their rejection on these grounds looms larger the more we look at it from the revolutionary prespective of those second-class citizens who surrounded Jesus throughout his life, who shared his table and whom he called 'blessed'.

The hungry of the Third World have raised awareness of what their theologians call the collective guilt of the First World in maintaining those systems and structures which make starvation inevitable for some. Those who go hungry at our Eucharists raise a similar awareness in the Christian churches about discriminatory structures. These institutionalize the injustice of withholding true bread for life from those not recognized as worthy. Our collective responsibility for this is re-emphasized by those who sit in the pews while we are fed.

The hungry of the Third World and the hungry at our Eucharists should be an insistent reminder of the vital connection between hunger, bread and life. The relationship between them must be kept intact if our companionship, our eating bread together, is to be a true experience of life shared in Christ.

In our industrialized corner of the globe, never-failing food supplies are taken for granted. Eating can become a matter of ritual rather than of hunger. So also with the Eucharist.

Pictures from Sudan or Ethiopia may remind us that, for the hungry, food forces itself forward as an insistent need, an insistent symbol of life sustained or destroyed. But our consumer-glutted society keeps us safely at one remove from hunger's savage insistence. This makes possible a collective psychic numbing in our churches whereby the Eucharist is used as a symbol of each church's power to minister rather than as life-sustaining bread for all.[10]

The starvation of those rejected by discriminatory Church practices is not finally a matter of life and death for them. In the ultimate analysis of structures, that described in Matthew's parable of the Last Judgment (Matt. 25:31–46), those who go hungry at our Eucharists reveal the eternal condemnation of those who fail to feed them. Arguments about ministry, worthiness, real presence or education are not taken into account by this Judge. The only evidence which counts in our favour is a compassionate reaction to the need of others. Those who cannot produce it are condemned to the eternal absence of God.

So the hungry by their very presence and protest become a prophetic disruption of the prevailing Eucharistic order. They remind us that our gifts are unacceptable at the altar while our sisters and brothers have a grievance against us. They force us to question a distribution of resources which is based on the 'worthiness' of some rather than the neediness of all.

This is the kind of disruption forced on Judaeo-Christian structures time and again by the presence of those classic figures, the widow and orphan, the starving and imprisoned, the stranger, the sick and the naked. They are all synonyms for powerlessness and neediness. The Latin American experience has shown that in some cases the churches receive this prophetic challenge and are transformed. In others, they shore up the walls to preserve the achieved forms of unity and security.

Similar reactions can be expected wherever church

structures appear threatened by the witness of the poor to the indiscriminate love of God. To put visible eucharistic justice on the agenda demands a radical change in practice that leaves churches open and vulnerable. Such change comes from the realization that it is the Father, not ecclesiastical bounty, who daily gives us all true bread from heaven. In justice to God, we must not thwart this intention. We realize too that before God we are all poor, all welcome, and all worth dying for. Then the Eucharist becomes the place where we give thanks for both our value and our neediness. In union with the open hands of the poor, we accept that we can have no option about sharing bread with all needy Christians.

The mystery of our common life and death expressed in the sharing of bread is summed up in a true story told by a survivor of Auschwitz. In a radio interview forty years later, she was asked the question which haunts all who survived the Holocaust: 'Why did you survive when so many died?' She anwered by re-living the moment of her arrival at the camp. Forcibly separated from her family, she was stripped, shaved, bathed, given a shapeless garment to put on and then shoved into a barn-like building where she was confronted by a terrified group similarly shaven and clad. Fright and desolation over-whelmed her. Then a girl broke out of the group, came over and thrust a piece of bread into her hand. 'At that moment,' she said, 'I decided to live.'

CHAPTER 1

The Witness of Disciples

THE PROPHETIC DISRUPTION of the prevailing order by the poor is a liberative moment for those who belong to that order. It is also a destabilizing moment. It upsets the perspectives and patterns through and in which we see our world, and in this instance, our eucharistic companionship. The conventional hierarchical structures and the accepted practices are assaulted. One bastion in particular has to be demolished if we are to be free to witness at our celebrations to the all-inclusive love of God. This is the separation of the 'worthy' from the 'unworthy'. The main weapon of attack is the rediscovery of Jesus himself as *the* prophetic disruption of conventional separatedness in his own day and within his faith tradition. There are two main areas in his life where this can be seen. One is his teaching in parables. The other is his scandalous behaviour in eating and drinking with tax-collectors and sinners. In both, to use Sally McFague's words, 'he epitomizes the scandal of inclusiveness for his time'.[1]

The rest of this book will be taken up with an exploration of this scandalous behaviour. This will, it is hoped, make possible a change of consciousness in the way we approach our Eucharists. No longer are we looking for ways of elevating the 'unworthy' or demoting false worthiness. Rather, by concentrating on the non-elevated status of Jesus' own breaking of bread at ordinary meals, we find ourselves with a radically different viewpoint of worthiness. It is inclusive instead of exclusive.

15

Through the interaction of these two viewpoints a tension is created which makes it necessary and possible for us to rediscover and redescribe the true character of our own breaking of bread.

To begin with, we shall take a story from John's Gospel, Chapter 4, in which Jesus figures plainly as a disruptive force on his own and a neighbour's tradition. This is his encounter with the Samaritan woman, in which his natural need for food sparks off a progressively shocking series of actions and dialogues. His egalitarian behaviour toward the woman forces both her and his disciples to re-assess their normal codes of conduct. It is after this experience that the woman bears witness to Jesus among her Samaritan kinsfolk.

The narrative opens with Jesus and his disciples passing through Samaria on their way to Galilee. Jesus says he is weary and sits down by a well. His disciples, who have been baptizing, go to buy food, as he is obviously both hungry and thirsty. A Samaritan woman comes to draw water and Jesus asks her for a drink. Jews, it is explained, have no dealings with Samaritans, so she is astonished that he should ask for a drink from her, and says so. Samaritan women were considered doubly unclean—indeed the term itself was synonymous with uncleanliness.[2]

Jesus answers the woman by saying that if she knew who she was talking to, she would ask him for living water and he would give it to her. She misunderstands: he has no jar and the well is deep; how would he get it? Is he greater than Jacob who gave the well to the Samaritans? Jesus replies that whoever drinks the well water will thirst again, but whoever drinks the water that he will give will never thirst. The woman asks him for this water, 'that I may not thirst, nor come here to draw'.

The geography of the story places the well at about a mile from the city, and this was the sixth hour—noon—the heat of the day. Jesus was identifying with the despised classes such as women and Samaritans who have to labour during unsocial hours to keep thirst at bay.

Jesus tells the woman to call her husband, and she replies that she has none. Jesus agrees: she has had five, and the present one is not her husband. The woman realizes that he knows things about her even though he has never seen her before. As Nathanael had done, she responds to his miraculous knowledge by acknowledging him as a prophet.

The ensuing conversation between them contains some of the most profound statements in the Gospels. The Father is to be worshipped in spirit and in truth; God is spirit; she confesses Jesus to be the Messiah and he receives and endorses her confession.

When the disciples return they are astonished to find him talking to a woman. The evangelist underlines the extraordinary nature of the meeting. C.K. Barrett tells us that there is no parallel to this incident in the Synoptic Gospels, 'though Luke's special interest in Samaritans and women (as in other despised classes) [*sic*] may be compared'.[3] It seems even more to the point to say that *Jesus* has a special interest in Samaritans, women and other despised classes, and thus the astonishment of the disciples at his conduct is noted for posterity. The woman leaves her water jar from which Jesus has drunk, goes to the city and says to the people: 'Come and see a man who told me all I ever did. Is he not the Christ?' There is another echo here of Philip's call to Nathanael (John 1:45).

While the Samaritans are on their way to him, the disciples urge him to eat, but he refuses, telling them that his real food is to do the will of God. Then, we are told, 'Many Samaritans from that city believed in him *because of the woman's witness*'. The Greek word used here for witness has already been used of John the Baptist (John 1:7). Barrett comments: 'To bear witness is the task of a disciple. The woman joins with John the Baptist as witness, and in fact precedes the apostles.'

The re-discovery of her discipleship does not depend only on her playing the same role as John the Baptist. The evangelist uses the technical New Testament Greek verb for 'labour'–*kopian* (cf. 1 Cor. 15:10; 16:16)–when Jesus describes the woman's missionary work to the disciples: 'I have sent you to reap what you have not laboured for. Others have laboured and you have come to enjoy the fruits of their labour.' The common rejoicing of sower and reaper could mean that Jesus is identifying with the woman rather than with the disciples. As he has laboured with her, and she with the Samaritans, now they are reaping together the harvest of the believing Samaritans. These would become the foundation of the flourishing Samaritan Church recorded in Acts 8 and 9.

While providing a clear statement of the discipleship of equals called forth by Jesus, this narrative can also be read as part of his Kingdom vision. In the Kingdom parable of the Last Judgment Jesus is identified with those who are oppressed in the present (Matt. 25:31–46). In his relationship with the Samaritan woman, this identification is made plain. He introduces himself to her as one who is thirsty, and she gives him something to drink. That is the kernel of the story. Read in conjunction with Matthew 25, it becomes a challenging and shocking statement about the presence of the Kingdom and who can claim part in it.

The woman responds to Jesus' need by leaving her waterpot there for him while she returns to the city, even though she would be justified in refusing him a drink because of the scorn heaped on her by his fellow Jews. Her compassion for him springs from her own experience of thirst and not from any hope of a heavenly reward. She identifies with him in his need; he identifies her with those who are blessed because 'I was thirsty and you gave me drink'. Matt. 25:31–46 is a parable of judgment because it reverses expectations of who is blessed and why. As in the other parable about a Samaritan (Luke 10:26ff), the despised outsider is the one who keeps the Law and is

18

blessed for it. She also shows up the failure of the official representatives of orthodoxy to recognize its demands. The condemned in Matthew 25 protest that they did not even see Jesus. The disciples forget Jesus' need for a drink in their shock at his receiving one from such a woman.

This dislocation or inversion of values which makes its bite felt in the parables is precisely their value in a theology which demands a radical change of outlook. This change calls for a move from immaturity to maturity in the Spirit. In the ecumenical context, it calls for a move from the oppressive security of Church pronouncements on full communion to a liberating insecurity. This freedom chooses to show love and to minister to the hunger and thirst of others regardless of their status or orthodoxy. Christ and the heretic woman drank out of the same vessel from the same well.

To the Jews, the Law of Moses was the 'Gift of God'. Jesus' relationship with Samaritans shows that the Law is truly understood only by those who interpret its demands (or if need be transform them) to benefit someone in need. More, he gives us a model for a humility which is prepared to receive God's gifts from those one has been taught to despise. If a heretic, and a woman at that, can meet Jesus' needs by ministering to him, what does this say to those of his Church who refuse to recognize each other's ordained ministry? But neither is there comfort here for fundamentalist Protestants who are indifferent– or indeed positively antagonistic–to sharing the Eucharist with Catholic Christian denominations.

This example of what Jesus' companionship meant in his own time, with the new complexion it gives to our Eucharists, is summed up for us by Juan Luis Segundo. He is in fact speaking of Jesus' demand for a change of outlook among those in Israel who declare officially what is the will of God. By substituting 'Church' for 'Israel' his conclusion can be applied to legal traditions about full communion:

Not only does Jesus point out that (human) legalistic traditions have been taking the place of God's authentic commandments. He also asserts that even the latter considered 'apart from' the human being, do not constitute the will of God as a generator of moral values (Mark 7:1–23). God does not come to human beings with pre-established moral recipes. He wants them to establish their morality in accordance with their intentions–freely, from within themselves and accepting the risk entailed. And to say it once again: only those whose intentions are based on love correctly understand the useful sense of the Commandments.[4]

In the light of all this, how can church representatives fail to hear the solemn warning to them contained in the words: 'I was hungry and you gave me no food, I was thirsty and you gave me no drink'?

Long familiarity with the Samaritan woman's story may at first dull our sense of shock at it. However, we must re-discover the outrage originally felt if we are to recover its meaning for us in the light of our own time. The narrative alternately reveals and conceals the outrage. At a first reading the woman's shock is understandable; so is that of the disciples. But these obvious reactions conceal the real scandal to them all which successive readings reveal. The first shock is evident in the amazement of the woman herself at being accosted by an orthodox Jewish man. She knew the implacable hostility between Jew and Samaritan. This centuries-old antagonism had reached a new peak in her lifetime. Josephus records that at one Passover betweeen AD 6 and AD 9 some Samaritans had strewn human bones in the Temple Sanctuary in the middle of the night. This appalling act of revenge which interrupted the Passover Feast by defilement had added fresh fuel to the fires of hatred. More to her amazement, Jesus asks a favour of her. More astonishing still, his knowledge that she has been the mistress of five successive men calls forth no condemnation from him. On the contrary, he does the unthinkable: he drinks from the water jar of a Samaritan adulteress. To the Jews, such a vessel would have been ritually unpurifiable.

Even without her adultery a Samaritan woman was considered perpetually unclean, and this resulted in anything she touched being levitically unclean. Jesus' breaking down of barriers between Jew and Samaritan, male and female, prophet and sinner, clean and unclean, makes her question him about the greatest barrier between them–that between Mount Gerizim and Mount Zion. This was the battleground between the Jews and the Samaritans for possession of God's chosen place. The reigning High Priestly family in Jerusalem was descended from John Hyrcanus, who had destroyed the Samaritan Temple in Gerizim in BC 129. The time will come, Jesus says to her, when God the Father will not be worshipped by discriminating Samaritans on Mount Gerizim or by discriminating Jews in Jerusalem, but in spirit and in truth–that is, everywhere. The destruction of this final barrier is for her the most devastating revelation of all. But the shock of it is transformed into joy that she has found the Christ, the Saviour of all. This joy sends her back to witness to him in her own city.

There is a beautiful icon of this scene. At the top left-hand corner are the disciples returning with food. At the top right-hand corner are the Samaritans emerging from their houses. Both groups are looking down at the bottom centre of the icon where Jesus and the woman are deep in conversation under the canopy of the well.[5] It must be one of the few icons which depict the disciples looking down on Jesus. But their attitude rightly places them on the same level as the woman's Samaritan kinsfolk, who hasten to tell her that their conversion no longer depends on *her* witness.

The disciples, no less than the woman, marvelled at Jesus' conduct–that he was actually giving a woman instruction about the Father and how to worship him.

According to Rabbi Eliezer it was 'better to burn the Torah than to teach it to women'. Professor R. Meyer points out that 'neither the Old Testament nor the Mishnah knows the feminine form of the Hebrew adjectives, pious, just and holy'.[6]

Nevertheless, not one disciple questions him directly, as she had done. Perhaps they were afraid of the implications of his possible answers. They must have heard John the Baptist witness that 'he whom God has sent utters the words of God, for it is not by measure that he gives the Spirit' (John 3:32f). The Baptist had promised that Jesus would give the Spirit without measure. Jesus measured neither the Gift nor the recipient. Even having heard this the disciples still expected him to behave according to the legalistic traditions of Israel. They simply could not conceive that Jesus had offered this woman Living Water, which in John's Gospel is a symbol of the Gift of the Spirit (cf. also 1 Cor. 12:13).

If any of his modern-day disciples reading this account do not experience the scandal of Jesus' conduct, they have not understood the context properly. For unless we empathize with the outrage felt then, we fail to be shocked today when some of his disciples still cannot accept that Jesus offers his Spirit as freely to women as to men. Or rather, they cannot accept what must follow from this.

How many in the church today really believe that God's Spirit is poured out without measure so that both sons and daughters may prophesy? This fundamental premise not only insists on the value of each individual regardless of gender; it also recognizes the value of each and every Christian in the Church at large. If this is the case, no discrimination can be justified. Christ's promise of the Spirit without measure, to all, enables us to accept and share the discipleship of equals with other Christian churches.

The power to witness which frees men and women equally to become disciples must be Trinitarian. It witnes-

22

ses to one Church which lives by the Word and in the
power of the Spirit. A Trinitarian basis for witness guards
against the narrowness of an institutional church which
sees the bishop alone as representing Christ to the church
just as Christ represents God, and which sees that
institution alone as having a mission of salvation to fulfil
in the world. Such a notion of Church confines the Spirit
(in every sense) to the ordained ministry. Rather, it is
important to stress the fundamental role of the Holy Spirit
at every level of the Church. In this way, the sending of
the Son into the world through the Spirit by the Father is
the creative force behind a witnessing Church. All will be
impelled to witness to the truth that all are loved
indiscriminately.

In Jesus' farewell address to the disciples (John 14:15ff)
this insistence on our common maturity in the Spirit is
highlighted by the distinction made by Jesus himself
between the disciples' dependence on him while he is
alive, and the independence in the Spirit which he desires
for them. The living union of Jesus and his disciples in
faith is most clearly symbolized in the figure of the vine
and the branches–the sharing of one nature and one life.
Jesus prays for the perfection of this life in them and
promises that they will receive it when he departs. As long
as he is with them they depend on him, the linchpin of
their lives, but after his departure, the Spirit will be their
direct connection with God. The Spirit of God will animate
their entire being, making the truth of Jesus known to
them and giving them the power to proclaim it and the
grace to live by it.

This life lived in Trinitarian relationship creates a
community united in love, a community which everyone
may recognize as Christian. Jesus gave his life in love for
his friends. His love has no limits, so the community
united in it will set no bounds either to their love. This
love is not simply a concept: it cost Jesus his life. He made
no secret of the cost to his disciples too. United in it, we

stand in the shadow of the Cross and of the Crucified. In his life he was the friend of sinners; on the Cross he was identified with the despised and the disregarded for one last and terrible time. It is our identification with the suffering Christ which reminds us that 'martyr' and 'witness' are the same word in Greek; our identification with the suffering Christ enables us to suffer the pains of immaturity and insecurity–perhaps the pain of being publicly identified with the outcast, the heretic and the schismatic.

But the Spirit of the Son of God can transform even that pain into resurrection joy. Jesus' final identification with the thirsty, on the Cross, makes it possible for us all to share the cup of blessing and to drink the new wine of resurrection in the Kingdom.

CHAPTER 2

The Witness of Jesus

IN HIS QUEST for the Golden Fleece, Jason sent a dove to find the way through the Wandering Rocks which floated and constantly crashed into each other. The dove chose its moment carefully and got through, losing only the tip of its tail. The Argonauts followed it and also got through unscathed but for some minor damage to the stern of the Argo.

Brendan O'Regan, Chairman of the Irish Peace Institute, recalls this story when writing about the search for a solution to the many conflicts of Northern Ireland, Britain, Europe and the Third World. The way forward, he says, is blocked by the sheer rock face of Scylla–'the way of hard dogmatic facts, ideologies and creeds'–and by the whirlpool of Charybdis–'the way of protest, whether that of the pacifist or the terrorist'. The challenge of the Wandering Rocks is made up of 'misunderstanding, distrust, fear and hate'. The dove, he points out, has always been a symbol of peace, and once the decision has been made to follow in its path, then 'we could find these rocks dissolving in the very ferment created by our own determination to get through in spite of them'.[1]

This valuable insight speaks directly to us in our search for a breakthrough in the stalemate created and reinforced by eucharistic discrimination. Even the attempts to end it can exacerbate the problem: Lukas Vischer has spoken, for instance, of how much resentment there is within the World Council of Churches about Rome's policy of working on ecumenical statements with selected churches

25

only. Paper qualifications for full communion ought not to take precedence over Christ's invitation to us all.

The Scylla of hard dogma presents a daunting prospect regardless of the tradition on which it is based. While Anglicans declare that the Roman Catholic Mass contains 'blasphemous fables, and dangerous deceits' (Article 31), and while Roman Catholics deny the validity of Anglican Orders, the heights must remain unscalable. The obstacle is reinforced by having for its foundation two immovable rocks: the infallibility of scripture and the infallibility of the pope. Unfortunately, it is against this impregnable bastion of dogma that most ecumenical effort is directed and consequently shattered. John Coventry writes: 'Many years of listening in, and occasionally contributing to, inter-church discussions on ministry, and in sharing in the shipwreck of endeavours lasting from Lambeth 1920 to the collapse of church unity negotiations in England in 1980 on the rocks of "ministry"—all this convinced me that light must come from a different quarter.'[2]

The Charybdis of protest does not loom so large, perhaps because official ecumenical church bodies do not have it in their sights. Nevertheless, it assumes a terrifyingly visible form in the conflict of Northern Ireland. It is a hidden menace in some Central American states. In Europe as a whole it is concealed under the cloak of indifference, of refusal to expend energy in a useless task, of silent withdrawal from sectarian isolation. But whether overtly violent or repressed, the protest is generated by a sense of oppression. Individuals and groups are oppressed by Church policies which give a higher priority to 'good order' than to justice. Injustice to fellow human beings in the name of any particular church can generate a violent reaction in those who suffer the injustice (for example, the Protestant policy: 'No Jews or Catholics need apply'), or a negative reaction in those who cannot stomach being identified with the injustice. Increasingly, the injustice of being denied access to Christ's table in the name of 'good order' is generating protest from the laity, but protest which is largely silenced by official church pronouncements.

We are sucked into the deep whirlpool of silent protest when, for instance, Christians of different denominations marry. Very often the couple decide to forego the Nuptial Mass which would be standard practice at a Roman Catholic wedding, in order to avoid the 'embarrassment' of a Communion Service which openly excludes many of the guests. The early Church used the same word, *koinonia*, for the union of Christ with the Father, of the Church with Christ and of flesh with flesh in marriage. The generosity with which the couple give themselves to each other finds no reflection in their respective churches. The sharing of their worldly goods with each other finds no counterpart in the Church's distribution of its resources. The result is that the bride and bridegroom are forced to withdraw from full communion. They suffer the injustice of their communion with each other not being given its complete expression in communion with the Body and Blood of Christ. The oppression of divided loyalties at the very outset of their marriage can wrench them gradually from their respective churches or even from each other.

Along with the hazards of Scylla and Charybdis, we who seek church unity must also face the challenge of the Wandering Rocks. These lie in wait for us in rough seas but, as Segundo reminds us, the moments of greatest activity and creativity, both in individual and collective history, are those of crisis.[3] Self-awareness and maturity are the fruits of conflict, of the response to challenge described by O'Regan as the ferment created by our determination to fight misunderstanding, distrust, fear and hate. He sees the dove of peace as the guide for choosing the correct path and for judging the right moment to take it. He calls this 'the Third Way'.[4] We have the same guide, but with a different name. The Spirit which hovers over the waters seeking a way through, is Holy Spirit. We call the way ahead the way of the Trinity.

This same Spirit led Jesus into the wilderness; it equipped him for his mission at his baptism; it gave him power to heal the sick, to convert Samaritans and to raise to life all who believe in him.

Where does the Spirit lead us? It leads us into truth which makes us free; it equips us with power to love; it gives us ability to recognize the suffering and rejected Jesus as the loving Father's Son. Therefore: 'Without him, but not without his Spirit, we must find out what he would say to free us if he were alive today!' (cf John 16:13; 1 Cor. 2:9ff).[5]

Jesus himself reminds us how costly and difficult our journey is (Matt. 16:24f). But as with the Wandering Rocks, we find the way ahead when we confront the difficulties. We shall do this by centering our attention on the mystery of his indiscriminate love for sinners.

The Spirit particularly reveals the identity of Jesus as the indiscriminate love of God incarnate in the encounter between him and a woman in the house of Simon the Pharisee. All four Gospels recount the story (Luke 7:36f; Matt. 26:6f; Mark 14:3f; John 12:1f). Close attention to the detail and variation in each account clears our vision of Jesus from what Segundo calls 'all the false pretensions of human beings. . . to grab hold of him, box him in universal categories and thus strip him and his Cross of their bite and scandal'.[6]

In Luke's account, the sinful woman washes his feet with her tears, wipes them with her hair and anoints them with spikenard. Jesus leaves her free to express her love and her contrition. Simon the Pharisee reacts to this 'freedom' on Jesus' part–being free with forgiveness to such a woman, free with his person, free with the Law– by using the Law to judge both Jesus and her. Simon's argument runs thus: if Jesus were a prophet he would recognize this woman for what she is, a sinner, and behave according to the Law by keeping a proper distance from her. Further, if he says he forgives sins, he is not only breaking the Law but blaspheming against it, for according to the Law only God can forgive sins.

This illustrates perfectly what Segundo means by 'boxing in' Jesus. Simon the Pharisee measures him against the 'box' of the Law, and finds he does not fit. This makes it impossible for him to recognize Jesus as a Prophet. In John 7:49 the Pharisees' disbelief in Jesus is contrasted with the belief of 'the crowd who do not know the Law'.

In the other three Gospels the disciples' response is no better. Their morality under the Law assesses the monetary value of what the woman has 'wasted' on Jesus and judges that it should have been spent on good works according to the Law, on alms to the materially poor. So they share Simon the Pharisee's inability to accept Jesus, scandalized by his attitude to a sinful woman and his assumption of the power to forgive. Luke puts them together as 'those who were at table with Him'.

Matthew heightens the irony by placing the whole scene after the decision of the Chief Priests and Caiaphas that Jesus had to die, and the decision of Judas to betray him. This failure to recognize Jesus as the loving Father's Son by 'one of the Twelve' is part of their common failure as disciples. John's Gospel echoes the story in the course of the Passion narrative, and highlights their shortcomings by putting their 'moral' reaction into the mouth of Judas alone.

We can see from the reactions of those at table with Jesus how any law made into an absolute renders even good acts *unlawful*. Jesus himself calls the woman's action 'a beautiful deed'. But for the Pharisees and the disciples it is scandalously sinful. Their vision of Jesus is impaired by the letter of the Law; so is their view of other people's actions.

Those at the meal were boxed in by their own expectations of the Law, of God, and of themselves, so that they could recognize neither Jesus, nor the true nature of sin, nor the true value of their own and others' deeds. The ability to enlarge this tunnel vision is the gift of the Spirit. Paul states this clearly: 'So my brothers, the death of Christ on the Cross has made you "dead" to the claims of the Law... and we are free to serve God not in the old obedience to the letter of the Law, but in a new way, in the Spirit' (Rom. 7:4–6). This re-emphasizes the need for us to move from the oppressive security of the Law to a liberating insecurity in the Spirit; from pre-established moral recipes to intentions based on love. Paul's 'new way' is the way of the Trinity.

By keeping the spirit of God's Law we are enabled to recognize who Jesus really is. 'Every spirit which confesses that Jesus Christ has come in the flesh is of God' (1 John 4:2). No one can say Jesus is Lord except by the Spirit. We must keep in mind the distinction Jesus himself made in his farewell address, between dependence on him and the independence in the Spirit which he desires for us (John 14:15). After his death Mary Magdalen was adjured not to cling to him. The very closeness of the disciples to him, their desires and expectations of him, prevented them from recognizing him. His death enabled them to receive his Spirit that would lead them into all truth. And through Jesus' Spirit, handed on to them at his death, they received their independence from himself, and with it the capacity to recognize his witness to the indiscriminate love of God. This maturity in the Spirit was not something given once for all, but was to grow as they realized it in their own lives with every responsible action, every free choice, every decision. In time, they could even make the momentous decision to admit Gentiles into the New Covenant.

The sinful woman did not base her hopes and expectations on the Law. She expected condemnation from it, ostracism from the righteous and contempt from ordinary hard-working people. She was a sinner: one of the accursed crowd who do not know the Law. She was excluded from the Temple and its liturgy, she was unable to contract an honest marriage and she was an occasion of sin to those who wished to remain cultically pure. As with the Samaritan woman, her very touch had to be wiped out by purification rites. When she entered the room, the disciples and the Pharisee together would have drawn back in righteous male solidarity against her.

The idea of pollution by association with women has not died out with the Pharisees. It is alive and well in many Christian churches. The Anglican Archbishops' Commission Report of 1936 on the ordination of women stated: 'We maintain that the ministration of women will tend to produce a lowering of the spiritual tone of Christian worship.' Fifty years on this view may not be so bluntly stated but it is a contributory factor in Anglican opposition to the ordination of women.

The downgrading of women rests on many ancient and modern taboos, but generally in Judaism and Christianity it reflects an ambivalent attitude towards sex and blood. Menstruating women and women in childbirth were untouchable in Judaism for seven days and forty or even eighty days respectively. St Augustine was convinced that 'nothing so casts down the manly mind from its height as the fondling of a woman'.

These views, which some churches have inherited consciously or not–'churching' of women after childbirth went on until recently–underlie their insistence on a celibate clergy, and as a corollary to that, a male clergy only. When Peter Damian discussed clerical marriage in the eleventh century he called clergy wives 'bitches, sows, screech-owls, she-wolves, blood suckers, harlots and prostitutes'. He urged clergy to kill such women. He was quoted by as recent a pope as Pius XII as an authority on clerical celibacy.

At the present time the Russian Orthodox Church has

threatened to leave the World Council of Churches if the demand made by women to participate becomes too powerful. The institutional downgrading of women is now a bargaining counter to be used in the name of 'ecumenical' unity. Women are presented as an 'obstacle' to this–yet the very word 'ecumenical' calls for the inclusion of all the inhabited world, a process which cannot flourish at the cost of consciously excluding the female presence from altar and pulpit.

It is encouraging to read that some fifty bishops of the Episcopal Church of the United States have seen through this sham ecumenism. They decided that the non-recognition in England of women Anglican priests from other parts of the world made it necessary for them (the bishops) to decline as a matter of conscience from presiding at the Eucharist during the Lambeth Conference of 1988.

Returning to Luke's account of the scene in Simon's house, full weight must be given to the justifiable scorn of the Pharisee and the disciples if we are to feel the scandal of the woman's action and Jesus' reaction. We are so used to seeing Jesus' relationship with women and sinners as 'all right' that we may not see how completely 'all wrong' it would have seemed at the time–and in the eyes of some of his followers today would seem so still. Jesus' witness to her and through her of the indiscriminate love of God was, and still is, scandalous. The Pharisee and disciples recognized her as a sinner and expected him to reject her. Jesus also was aware of her sinfulness, yet did not reject her. As in his encounter with the Samaritan woman, this amazed the disciples and upset their expectations of Jesus as a law-abiding Jew. It gave the woman too a different expectation of him and she behaved accordingly.

Joachim Jeremias interprets her actions: to kiss a person's knee or foot is a sign of the most heartfelt gratitude, such as a man might show to one who had saved his life. Jeremias gives the example of a man accused of murder kissing the feet of the lawyer to whom he owes his acquittal. He goes on to say that Hebrew, Aramaic and Syriac have no word for 'thank' and 'thankfulness'. The context determines the word used to imply gratitude. Here it is 'grateful love'. He translates Jesus' words about her: 'God must have forgiven her sins, many as they are, since she displays such grateful love'. He concludes that 'Only the poor can fathom the full meaning of God's goodness'.

Matthew places the scene at the beginning of the Passion, immediately after the parable of the Last Judgment in which the truly righteous are astonished to find that they are inheriting the Kingdom because they have done such ordinary things as giving drink to the thirsty and welcoming the stranger. Luke gives us Jesus' dialogue with Simon in which he expressly charges Simon with *not* welcoming him. The sinful woman has fulfilled this condition for entry into the Kingdom by her grateful love. So who here is truly righteous and who is a sinner?

The woman receives no judgment based on the Law from Jesus, for the Law would unhesitatingly judge her the sinner and Simon the righteous one. The difference is summed up by Jesus: 'You judge according to the flesh. I judge no one' (John 8:15). She can hope not only that she will not be rejected by Jesus under the Law, but also that she might be accepted as his table companion. Other sinners had been. In Luke's account, the spirit in which the Pharisee invited Jesus becomes apparent when the woman follows him into the house. He had received none of the customary courtesy due to a guest from a host. The drama of the scene juxtaposes the sinners (Jesus and the woman) with the righteous (the rest of the company). We have already seen Jesus identified with the heretic Samaritan woman; now his identification with sinners is complete: 'This man receives sinners and eats with them' (Luke 15:2). It is this, ultimately, which makes necessary

33

in the eyes of the Sanhedrin his condemnation and death as a sinner under the Law. Only when Jesus had gone to the Father would the Spirit come who would 'convince' the world of sin, of justice and of judgment (John 16:8ff), and only then would the disciples accept their own unrighteousness.

The woman did not expect Jesus to declare her righteous or to forget her sins. (The Samaritan woman knew that he recognized her as the mistress of five men.) It was precisely *as* a sinner that she found he had received her. She recognized him as she recognized herself in her sinfulness: because she loved much, she recognized the gracious, justifying, saving love of God by which a lovable person is created from a nobody. In the eyes of the 'righteous' world, the needy, the poor and the sinful were all 'non-persons'. She identified with these and therefore she experienced God's loving forgiveness. 'Blessed is he who knows the needy and poor' in himself–or rather, herself.

Jesus' response in Matthew and Mark is that the woman's act should be remembered as an act of extravagant love. It provides for the future Church a beautiful example of how to respond to the extravagance of God's love for the world given in Christ.

The woman recognized Jesus' table companionship with sinners as the extravagant love of God incarnate. This recognition was the gift of the Spirit, not the letter of the Law. Jesus had received this Spirit to preach the good news to the poor, and in the same Spirit, the poor responded–those who were poor in the eyes of the Law, of the righteous and of themselves. They reacted to the indiscriminate love with which God had first loved them. Both the Samaritan woman and this woman witnessed to it by word and deed.

The ability to recognize and witness to the indiscriminate love of God in Jesus' table companionship with sinners is still the gift of the same Spirit. Today, as then, the power of the Spirit enlarges the vision of Jesus' disciples. Thus we are able to look at our eucharistic practices, which discriminate against other Christians in the name of righteousness, and see such practices for the scandal they have become. Jesus scandalized his contemporaries by eating with sinners. We, 'the righteous', are a scandal to him and to each other when we exclude 'sinners' in his name.

The major block to our vision is the notion that the Eucharist is for those who are 'worthy', those who are 'sinless', those whose unity with each other is obvious and admirable. This block begins to move when we recognize our common unworthiness, our real sinfulness, our scandalous disunity as precisely that which brings us to his table. Recognition of the mystery of God's love for us *as sinners* is the only condition which Jesus imposed.

This gift of the Spirit calls forth a response from us. We open our hearts to a broader consciousness of eucharistic celebration and grow in awareness of what it meant to eat with Jesus. One of Jeremias's major works, *The Eucharistic Words of Jesus*, concentrates on the five Last Supper texts: 1 Cor. 11:23–5; Mark 14:22–5; Matt. 26:26–9; Luke 22:15–20; John 6:51–8. Yet Jeremias says it is a mistake to presuppose that the meals of the earliest Church were repetitions of this last meal with Jesus. He underlines the statement: '*The meals of the Early Church were not originally repetitions of the last meal which Jesus celebrated with his disciples, but of the daily fellowship of the disciples with him.*'[8]

There are consequences for eucharistic practice in basing it exclusively on the biblical accounts of Jesus' last meal. He is 'boxed in' with twelve male apostles as his sole companions. His actions and theirs on that particular occasion are ritualized as the only valid celebration of the New Covenant. All his other meals are telescoped into this last one. In this way the real scandal occurs: he is presented as the one who discriminates at his Father's table in favour of a few elite men, apparently excluding even his own mother. This scandalous stereotyping prevents people today from recognizing him as he was recognized in his own lifetime—as the one who welcomed sinners such as Mary Magdalen and Zacchaeus, was welcomed by them to meals and was reckoned among them because of it.

Discrimination against non-disciples and women (who are then assumed to belong in the same pigeon-hole) is not the only effect of using Jesus' last meal as the sole pattern of his table companionship. To call him a glutton and a drunkard, as he reported of himself, would never occur to anyone wandering in by chance to some of the meals celebrated in his Name today. Where is the joy, the bounteousness, the indulgence in the good things of life that such a phrase conjures up? Instead, the Eucharist has become a solemn affair on an entirely sacred plane, which proceeds along rigid lines towards a foregone conclusion.

But it is impossible to reconcile such Eucharists even with the accounts of Jesus' last meal from which the pattern is drawn. John concentrates on the washing of the disciples' feet and their preparation for the coming of the Spirit. Luke includes an unedifying squabble between the disciples about which of them shall be the greatest—and this is their response both to the words of institution and to the warning of betrayal.

Eucharistic celebrations have not remained faithful to the spirit of Passover celebrations either. In the Introduction to his order of service for Passover (the Seder), one rabbi makes a comment on how the Eucharist, even in a Passover model, has diverged from Jewish celebration. He remarks that many Jews are discouraged from holding the Passover because 'the freedom festival itself has become slavishly imprisoned in rigid form'. This view of the Seder, he says, as 'an untouchable ritual' is perhaps the result of a link between the Passover Seder and a Christian rite. He states: 'By reversal, this gives Jews the impression

that *just as a Catholic communion is a fixed ritual* so too must
be the Seder'(!) (our italics).

This fixed ritual nature of eucharistic celebrations
reinforces the notion that the Church's service belongs out
of this world, in a dimension beyond time, beyond history
and change, and that power of access to this higher plane
is 'vested' solely in the clergy. They alone dress diffe-
rently, their robes belonging to a different time and place,
making it more difficult for us to remember that the priest
travels the same journey as all humankind and shares the
same earthly lot with the world. But if we forget that, says
Segundo, then we make the mistake of thinking that the
history of the world and of the Church, of human effort
and of grace and salvation, are different floors in the same
building.[9] This mistaken division between Church and
world is driven deeper into our consciousness when the
clergy dress and behave as though they alone have access
to the upper room.

The scene in Simon's house shows the same presuppo-
sitions in operation: Pharisees and disciples inhabit a
different world from sinful women; there is no sharing of
worship or table. Sins are forgiven ritually in another,
spiritual, dimension, for which the ceremonies of the Day
of Atonement in the Temple are set aside. The woman's
conduct was a forcible and unwelcome reminder that
there is only *one* world where we sin and are forgiven, and
that it is located unmistakably in the same dimension as
eating, drinking, welcoming strangers and lavishing
resources on those we love.

Writing of the Spirit in John's Gospel, George Johnston
recalls the story of the Samaritan woman. Who can she
be, he asks, but the world in Samaritan dress? And it is to
her that Jesus says: 'God is spirit, and those who worship
must worship in spirit and truth.' Johnston concludes:
'Given all that, such worship cannot be sectarian, *world-
denying*, individualist and pietistic' (our italics).[10]

Simon the Pharisee and the disciples make it plain that, left to their own devices, they would never have allowed the woman in. The righteous make the rules which decide whether or not anyone may eat with them. Access to meals is determined by Law and ritual, and this ritual is governed by those with access to God's rightousness. In Luke 11, when another Pharisee invites Jesus to a meal, he expresses astonishment that Jesus did not wash ritually before eating. These rituals are detailed in Mark 7. In both Gospels Jesus gives one of the harshest reponses of his ministry, rejecting a tradition which differentiates between the outside of a man and the 'inside'–what is in the heart. 'You fools!' he says. 'Did not he who made the outside make the inside also?'

The parable of the Prodigal Son ends with the elder brother angrily refusing to go in and eat the fatted calf with his father. It would have meant sitting at the table with a brother who had 'devoured' their father's living with harlots. The elder brother is presented by Christianity as a jealous, perverse and blind man. Yet what is the reaction of many Christians today to sharing the cup with social and moral outcasts?

What, then, can be done about practices which deny access to the Eucharist on grounds of 'unworthiness'? The Roman Catholic Church practised an internal sanction for many years, encouraging attendance at the sacrament of Penance before receiving Holy Communion. Although this is no longer the tradition for adults, there are still places where children are required to make their First Confession before receiving their First Communion, thus perpetuating and reinforcing the notion that the righteous do not eat with sinners. This attitude Jesus opposed with his life. Proper use of the sacrament of Penance may foster the correct acceptance of one's sinfulness and nothingness before God, and of God's extravagant love which creates righteousness from it. But to present Penance as a means of making oneself worthy to receive the Eucharist is to misunderstand both sacraments. We are not referring here to cases where people have been barred from communion because of open scandal, but to the attitude that sinlessness is a requirement for eucharistic companionship.

Allied to this is the assumption that worthiness is mediated through a particular baptismal tradition. Recently, there was a tightening-up in eucharistic practice in the United States, when the Roman Catholic bishops urged their priests to make certain that those who received holy communion from them had been baptized in the Roman Catholic Church. In practice, of course, the pastors could only be certain of this if they required all communicants to produce baptismal certificates as they queued at the altar. The absurdity of the directive should not make us any less concerned about the kind of thinking from which it issues.

At the heart of such thinking is the assumption that righteousness is mediated through ritual, that such righteousness may be identified with one class of person as opposed to another, and that access to this righteousness is vested in the clergy. Because of these assumptions, the table companionship of Jesus has lost its true bite and scandal. The salt has lost its taste.

After Matthew's account of his own calling we read that many other tax collectors and sinners joined Jesus and his disciples for a meal. The Pharisees were appalled: tax collectors were traitors, employees of the hated Roman occupation forces, and were notorious for their dishonesty and avarice. Small wonder that they were invariably bracketed with sinners by the ethnically pure, Law-abiding Pharisees who saw themselves by contrast as righteous. To eat in such company was defilement, rendering a man unfit for Temple worship. Yet in spite of Jesus' unequivocal choice of self-confessed sinners as his table companions, there are still religious leaders today who assess themselves to be fit to take communion on the grounds of their worthiness. Then they use this assumption to turn away from the Eucharist the very people Jesus came to call to his table.

This brings us to the heart of the problem, into the midst of the Wandering Rocks. How can we truly recognize who Jesus is in the world for us today if he is boxed in by the excluding claims of churches which say they represent him? How can churches recognize him in one another if they use their power of access to deny eucharistic companionship to other Christians on the grounds of the 'unworthiness' of traditions other than their own?

The way forward is to accept the witness of his scandalously indiscriminate identification with sinners in table companionship. The bite and scandal of Jesus' life was its lack of discriminatioon. If he is the one who refuses to discriminate, then the scandal made evident by the impasse in ecumenism is that of Christian discrimination. The self-image and self-expectation of churches that make and interpret canons of righteousness for admission to eucharistic companionship are the submerged rock, the stumbling block (*skandalon*) on which ecumenical efforts founder. With the help of the Kingdom vision of Jesus, who welcomes us on the basis of the welcome we have given to the hungry and thirsty, this rock shatters. Quite different canons are to be observed, best seen in contrast to the ones currently used.

At one end of the spectrum we have the Pope saying that dissent from the magisterium poses obstacles to the reception of the sacraments. At the other we have some fundamentalist Protestants who reject Roman Catholics from fellowship because, they say, their Marian devotions put them on a par with Mormons and Muslims. Anywhere in between can be found the kind of attitude reported in a survey by an American Lutheran theological student. He went to a number of Lutheran church services dressed cleanly but informally in a sweat shirt and jeans, and found himself rejected in fact if not by declaration.

Few ushers acknowledged his presence at all; if they did, it was only to direct him to the back of the church.

The most consistent attitude towards inclusion in and exclusion from prayer and table today appears in the disconcerting experience of a Benedictine monk who travelled in the Christian East as a lay pilgrim and student. In some monasteries he was excluded from prayer and table because he was not a communicant of the Orthodox Church. In one instance this meant no entry into the church during services, and taking his meals alone. In another he could go into the services but had to stay in the vestibule between church porch and nave, and eat at his own table by the refectory door separated from monks and Orthodox guests.[11]

The justification for such exclusion was based on distinctions between orthodox, heretic and schismatic. Its distinctive feature is the consistent attitude towards sharing food. Ordinary meals, blessed bread and eucharistic host are all seen as valid expressions of companionship. Joachim Jeremias stresses this characteristic of the Oriental mind to which, he says, symbolic action means more than it does to us. For the Oriental, table fellowship is a fellowship of life. Therefore the acceptance of the outcasts into table fellowship with Jesus would immediately be understood as an offer of salvation to guilty sinners and as the assurance of forgiveness. Hence, he says, the passionate objections of the Pharisees: 'This man receives sinners and eats with them!' (Mark 2:16; Matt. 11:19. They held that the pious could have table fellowship only with the righteous and understood Jesus' intention of according the outcasts worth before God.[12] Jeremias's understanding of the Oriental mind makes even more scandalous the present-day practices of some Christian Oriental monks.

The Western monk was more fortunate in his experiences in Israel. He saw that there the fortress approach to ecumenism has had to be revised radically. In the

41

monastery of St Macarius he picked up a booklet which included this comment on Christian unity: 'It is certain that, should we divest ourselves of our individual "me" and our ecclesial "me" as much on the conscious as on the subconscious level, unity would without question become a reality.'

Self-image and self-expectation on the individual and ecclesial levels are barriers to full communion. They prevent us from identifying and recognizing Jesus in the assembly of his disciples today. Is he not, as the Reformed tradition teaches, the Host and the Meal? But is he not also identified with the sinners who hunger and thirst for the food? As such he is excluded then, kept waiting in the porch until the just woman or man recognizes his need.

Segundo is clear about the nature of this hunger, this 'mysterious presence' of Jesus. It is not that he suffers the same material want as the least of his brothers and sisters, but that he feels the compassion (literally, 'suffering with') that all true love produces. This transmits from the loved one to the lover all that is intolerable and inhuman in the situation he or she suffers. The Samaritan woman who laboured to keep thirst at bay recognized and had compassion on Jesus' thirst. The sinful woman in the Pharisee's house knew what it was to be rejected and poured forth her compassion for Jesus in prospect of his ultimate rejection in death, for 'the day of his burial'.

Led by the Spirit, we too may jettison our exclusive self-image and be free to see ourselves and others with the compassion of Kingdom vision. When this happens, there is a radical revision of the Eucharist. We turn from the altar and find Christ among the congregation, and particularly among those we have excluded. We recognize the fellow-suffering of Jesus in them.

Segundo does not consciously equate ecclesiastical discrimination and eucharistic injustice with the neglect of ordinary human hunger and thirst. But the Orthodox Christians in their very discrimination teach us that we cannot separate them either. Segundo's observations make an even deeper impact if we read them in the context of eucharistic exclusion. God, he says, is truly recognized (for who God is and for what God wants) when the individual is freed from his or her misery: 'Moreover, if this is not done, no matter how religious one is (see James 2:14–17; 1 John 4:20), that "mysterious presence" will be replaced by eternal absence: "Out of my sight, you condemned, into that everlasting fire. . . I was hungry and you gave me no food. . . ." '[13]

Debates about 'Real Presence' should rather be concerned with this eternal absence.

CHAPTER 3

The Witness of the Body

'EH LASS, WE'RE nowt special. We're just put on earth to make the numbers up!'

This piece of Yorkshire wisdom passed on from mother to daughter captures the view which many church members have of themselves. It also tallies with Jesus' description of those who come to his table. At another meal in a Pharisee's house he tells two parables of how his guests are chosen (Luke 14). In that of the Great Banquet, the usual norms of behaviour for both guest and host are contradicted. *All* the invited guests send excuses at the very moment when everything is prepared. Angered by this, the host sends his servant to bring in anyone who can be found. If he cannot eat with friends, he will eat with strangers. The numbers at his table must be made up.

How are they made up? The instructions to the servant repeat the command given in the other parable: invite the poor, the blind, the lame, the maimed—and since there is still room, those in the highways and byways.

The picture presented is so unlikely, so bizarre, that while we muse on its improbabilities we are liable to forget its setting. Not only is Jesus addressing 'the Pharisees watching him', who would recoil in horror from being identified with either host or guest in the story; he uses it as a retort to one sitting beside him. This man had taken up Jesus' statement about rewards in the next life for feeding the poor, maimed, lame and blind. 'Blessed is he who shall eat bread in the Kingdom of Heaven', exclaims this pious guest. This is the kind of practical morality he can understand. The good deed which is not repaid now will be a luncheon voucher in the Kingdom of God.

'But Jesus said to him. . .'

As so often, these words begin a saying of Jesus which will run completely contrary to the hearers' expectations. Jesus' vision of the Kingdom in the Great Banquet parable that follows does not discount the practical morality of the Pharisees, but puts it in perspective. Their morality, and indeed ours, is made relative to the fundamental morality of the Kingdom. In practice people have to make distinctions and choices; for instance, we look forward to being asked back by those who have visited us. But God does not limit invitations. God's gift of life is for every creature. Jesus underlines this distinction between God's hospitality and ours. God's love and morality are all-inclusive.

Such parables bring us up short before the boundless nature of God's love. The feeling of vertigo one might experience at the edge of a bottomless crater corresponds to the kind of shock which can be the immediate effect of parable. The head spins at the giddy depths of a Love which will not discriminate.

There is a Jewish parable along these lines which induces the same vertigo:

God showed Moses the great treasure troves in which are stored up the various rewards for the pious and the just, explaining each separate one to him in detail: in this one were the rewards of those who give alms; in that one, of those who bring up orphans. In this way He showed him the destination of each one of the treasures, until at length they came to one of gigantic size. 'For whom is this treasure?' asked Moses, and God answered: 'Out of the treasures that I have shown thee I give rewards to those who have deserved them by their deeds; but out of this treasure do I give to those who are not deserving, for I am gracious to those also who may lay no claim to My graciousness, and I am bountiful to those also who are not deserving of My bounty.'[1]

Jesus made the same point in the parable of the Great Banquet. Those who taste the banquet do so because the host insists. The house is to be filled. This takes priority over everything else. There are no criteria for the guests: they can neither refuse nor repay hospitality. The poor, maimed, blind and lame are 'brought' in. Those in the highways and hedges are 'compelled'. These are the very categories forbidden the Sanctuary to offer bread to God (Lev. 21:18ff).

Nor does the invitation discriminate between those who belong to the city (the insiders, the Jews), and those beyond its gates (the outsiders, the Gentiles), except that the last mentioned (the tramps) are to be forced to come in and make up the numbers. Not only is there no discrimination between velvet, white and blue collars: some have no collars at all.

The shock of this parable began in the time of Jesus, like a rock thrown into a pool. The waves ripple out to disturb us today, and bring home the scandal embodied in the examples of church discrimination mentioned in the preceding chapter. Those *turned away* from our communion tables by present church canons of worthiness are exact counterparts of the guests *brought in* to the Great Banquet: they have no insider right of access, no properly completed baptismal certificates—perhaps not the right collars. And what welcome is there for those with bills of divorce in their pockets?

Yet those very churches which discipline the divorced as unworthy communicants are also found to *demand* divorce to establish worthiness. Writing of the mainline mission-founded churches in Africa, Kofi Asare Opoku says that they assume that one cannot sincerely love Christ and be a polygamist at the same time. Therefore they bar polygamists from the Lord's Supper *unless* the man divorces all his wives except the first. The sufferings which many people have gone through before being judged 'righteous' enough to partake of the Lord's Supper defy description:

> but the church considers this of little consequence, since in its view divorcing all one's wives and imposing untold hardship on many women and children is what Christ demands of those who love him.[2]

This distortion of Christ's demands has arisen, says Opoku, because the church uses the Lord's Supper as an instrument of discipline. Yet Jesus' own table companionship was condemned by the religious authorities of his day because it *broke* with discipline when he ate and drank with tax-collectors and sinners.

So what is the biblical authority, Opoku asks, for this exclusion which separates the 'righteous' (monogamist) from the 'unrighteous' (polygamists)? Does a person who has more than one wife necessarily cease to believe in Jesus as his Saviour? How can the church assert that such a person cannot believe in Jesus Christ?[3]

The shock we experience today when juxtaposing excluding church disciplines with the inclusive invitation of the Great Banquet parable, forces on our attention the failure of the churches to witness to the indiscriminate love of God. This is especially scandalous when, gathered publicly as Christ's body, we eucharistize, that is, give thanks for that love which we betray at the same moment.

But perhaps the deepest shock is felt when we face the mystery of our own invitation. We can make no claim on God's graciousness. So, have we no right to God's bounty? Must we be reckoned with the riff-raff, with those who have to be dragged in? Do we even want to be there, if the host will not distinguish between the good and the bad, the just and the unjust; if he distributes invitations as indiscriminately as sunshine and rain? Do we really believe Paul when he says: 'God has no favourites' (Roman 2:11)?

We are shocked by the contrast between our practical morality and the fundamental morality of the Kingdom. But the Kingdom vision of morality must be kept before us if we are not to find ourselves substituting our own for it. One criterion we can establish from this parable is our readiness to identify with the riff-raff of other denominations. Unless we accept that we are all 'nowt special' together, we risk our own invitation to table.

The fact that, humanly speaking, this is impossible, that our goal is beyond our reach, is both a remedy against downheartedness and a spur to further effort. Segundo points out that:

> No matter how many *signs* of its power may be firmly planted in history, there will always be a verifiable distance between embodiments of the kingdom and the kingdom itself. The laws of the easy way in an already created world will always be at work against the kingdom... Thus the task of constructing the kingdom with God, of taking the next step forward, will continue in all its radicalness from one generation to the next, challenging every individual and generation to display the full creativity of their love.[4]

Part of that task for us is to keep faith with the Kingdom vision of who is to be invited to Jesus' table. This keeping faith is a gift of the Holy Spirit which comes through prayerful reflection on Jesus' parables and actions. On the one hand the parables tell us that we are there to make the numbers up because our host so wills. On his initiative alone, we are drawn to his table indiscriminately. On the other hand, the host in the first parable practises positive discrimination. He *chooses* the poor, the blind, the maimed. But he has already chosen us. Can we accept the truth of the equation: ourselves = chosen poor? As the 'chosen', we are the poor, blind, maimed. What sort of elite is that?

Acceptance of this is particularly hard for those of us who are not materially poor. Our self-image seems to exclude need. Part of the problem of developing a liberation theology in the First World is its emphasis on improving the lot of the economically oppressed. A eucharistic liberation theology does not ignore economic deprivation, but redefines the concept of need within a eucharistic context. At God's table, those in velvet collars are just as needy as those without shirts. The vital link between hunger, bread and life draws us all to eat together. This is hidden from the materially rich as well as the materially poor by church practices which legislate for the eucharistic deprivation of some Christians in favour of others. Strategic classification by church author- ities of some as needy/worthy means the deprivation of others classed as needy/unworthy. Yet this is the only criterion that the God of Jesus applies.

It is equally hard for both classes to accept. But it must be accepted if, as well as listening to the parables, we look at Jesus' own practice. He did not demand a particular standard of poverty, a means test for those who wanted to eat with him. He refused to make any tests. More than that, he went looking for those who would never have presented themselves in the first place because they would be failed automatically. To the Jews of Jesus' day the rich Zacchaeus was as untouchable because of his occupation as the poor Lazarus of the parable because of his sores. Sin was as contagious as pollution. As a tax collector (synonymous with sinner) Zacchaeus was as ineligible a host as a diseased beggar would be a guest.

This idea of contagion is alien to our modern culture where class and religious conventions no longer control one another. Christians work alongside those of other beliefs or of no faith without fear of contamination. We invite whom we wish to our homes without preliminary screening. An 'open and notorious evil-liver' may offend, but no one sees his bad reputation as rubbing off on to others by physical contact, less still from a chair on which he has sat.

For the Jews, the table, the house and the Sanctuary

were centres of purity from which the impure and polluted must be excluded. If this was done, the food consumed in both the home and the Sanctuary brought a blessing. It brought life. If pollution entered the house or Sanctuary–and it was believed to come through touching someone or something impure–then contagion spread through the family or priesthood, and both family meal and sacrifice brought a curse. It brought death. Paul distinguishes between the cup of blessing (the cup of the Lord) and the cup of demons (1 Cor. 10:21). The Jewish ritual system depended on the distinction between the pure and the polluted, blessing and curse. It entailed ceaseless vigilance to preserve the purity of the table, the house and the Temple. Being Kosher was (and still is) a matter of life and death.

A similar attitude to pollution operates today at many levels outside Judaism. We accept that touch (contagion) is a system of transference for good or ill. Hygiene–personal, public and with food–is understood to be crucial for the battle against disease. Isolation wards and quarantine are necessary measures against contagion. Various taboos operate: the common one against using another's toothbrush has assumed nightmare significance in a world threatened by AIDS.

This principle of contagion works at other levels too. 'Is there any man here who is fearful and faint of heart? Let him go home lest he make his fellows lose heart also' (Deut. 20:8). Optimism and pessimism, heroism and panic are also 'catching'.

Moving on from our understanding of how 'bodies' affect one another, there is now a whole new rash of sciences dealing with the connections between mind and matter. Some of them are generated by the dramatic shift of basic concepts that has occured in modern physics. For example, the nuclear physicist Fritjof Capra presents us with a new vision of reality based on 'awareness of the essential interrelatedness and interdependence of all phenomena–physical, biological, psychological, social and cultural'.[5]

Though not expressed in these modern categories, the Jewish vision of reality which Jesus shared with his contemporaries had the same awareness. Like Capra's, it had a positive aim: the enhancing of the common life. But it differed in its view of how and why that interrelatedness and interdependence operated. The primary relation and dependence was between Yahweh and creation. Yahweh opens the heavens and the womb, makes the earth and the female fruitful. But even in this most intimate and life-giving relationship Yahweh is clearly separate. The Jewish scriptures' word for holy stems from the Hebrew word meaning to separate.

The essential difference between heaven and earth sums up for the Jew both the relation and the separation. Like heaven and earth, the pure and the impure must be kept separate, the pure being the proper space for fruitfulness, life, growth and blessing; the impure or polluted being the space of barrenness, death, destruction and curse. The necessary separation and intimate union between heaven and earth was the basis for the dietary and purity laws. 'Be holy, for I your God am holy', was a call to separate oneself from pollution. 'I call heaven and earth to witness against you this day, that I have set before you life and death, blessing and curse; therefore choose life, that you and your descendants may live' (Deut. 30:19).

This profound understanding of the relationship between Yahweh and Israel, heaven and earth, has been handed on to us by Paul:

> Do not unite yourselves with unbelievers; they are no fit mates for you. What has righteousness to do with wicked-ness? Can light consort with darkness? Can Christ agree with Belial, or a believer join hands with an unbeliever? Can there be a compact between the temple of God and the idols of the heathen? And the temple of the living God is what we are.

God's own words are: 'I will live and move about among them; I will be their God, and they shall be my people.' And therefore, 'come away and leave them; separate yourselves, says the Lord; do not touch what is unclean. Then I will accept you, says the Lord, the Ruler of all being; I will be a father to you, and you shall be my sons and daughters.' Such are the promises that have been made to us, dear friends. Let us therefore cleanse ourselves from all that can defile flesh or spirit, and in the fear of God complete our consecration (2 Cor. 6:14–7:1).

The relationship between Yahweh and Israel was the basis for 'cleansing ourselves from all that can defile'. The orthodox Jew did not measure his cleanliness in relation to other Jews *but in relation to Yahweh*. This logical sequence must be kept in mind if we are not to fall into the trap of thinking Judaism merely obsessive about cleanliness for its own sake. In his study of Paul and Palestinian Judaism, E.P. Sanders stresses how easy it is to miss this Jewish logic. When Paul says: 'the body is not meant for immorality, but for the Lord, and the Lord for the body', he is arguing that one participatory union can destroy another. Even though they are not on the same level, a person cannot participate in two mutually exclusive unions.

The proverbial mother-in-law illustrates this logic. A young couple marry and begin a relationship together which subtly moulds them into a new pattern of tastes, behaviour and values. The mother of one of them resents these changes, seeing them as threatening the bond with her child. If she clings to it with enough determination her child must either sever the familiar relationship with her, or the marriage union will be destroyed.

Sanders says that everyone agrees so readily with Paul that Christians should not commit sexual immorality, that it is easy to miss the logic behind it—logic that is foreign to us and natural to Paul:

We might expect an argument that a Christian should not behave in such and such a way, since immorality is not appropriate to being Christian, since it is forbidden in the Bible or since such a transgression will result in punishment from God; but to say that one should not fornicate because fornication produces a union which excludes one from a union which is salvific is to employ a rationale which today is not readily understood.[6]

Yet unless we try to understand the Jewish basis of keeping table fellowship 'pure', we fail to grasp the scandal of Jesus eating and drinking with the riff-raff of his day. We miss the logic of 'for our sake he made him to be sin who knew no sin, so that in him we might become the righteousness of God' (2 Cor. 5:21). We misunderstand the horror behind such questions as: '*Why* does your master eat with sinners?' and the certainty with which he was labelled as one in consequence: 'We *know* that this man is a sinner' (our italics). As Jesus placed his body in close proximity to 'polluted' bodies, he became polluted. As he shared table and house with sinners, he became one. His body ate the same food as sinners, received the unclean touch of a menstruating woman. His hands dipped into the bowl of the tax-collector; lifted the dead body of Jairus's daughter. This is why Paul says he was 'made sin'. He participated in the 'bodiliness' of sin, so that we might participate in his Body and drink of his Spirit.

Three things stand out here. First, the shock–which was quite unbelievable to any Jew–that God has become flesh, has taken a body. Heaven and earth are no longer separate. He came unto his own, and they did not receive him. But how could they? We cannot be complacent about our own ability to recognize and accept the body of Christ. When God is not 'boxed' in safe rituals or physically boxed in tabernacles, it is just as shocking to us as Jesus was to the Jews. That is why we have often confined him to a

Sanctuary from which only the cultically pure (clergy) may share his body with the cultically worthy (the 'properly' baptized and shriven).

Second, our efforts to maintain ritual purity have lost the sound basic premise of Judaism, which measures human purity not in relation to others but in relation to God. The Jews had as their ideal the holiness of God. This ideal required them to separate themselves from the unholy. But laws against intercommunion in Christian churches are based not on the unworthiness of all Christians, but of some compared to others. This is an absolute contradiction of Jesus' refusal to discriminate; literally a *saying against* his declaration that he came to seek and to save the lost. If we live with this contradiction and make it church policy, we lose sight of the basic premise of Christianity: he *alone* knew no sin, yet he did not separate himself from sinners. In relation to him, we are all unworthy and all welcome.

The third point follows from this: it becomes possible to understand how Jesus can be called the Parable of God.[7] He leads us to the edge of the abyss of God's love, where we discover that he is that edge. In his life and actions, summed up in his table companionship, he refused to separate himself from us. He is the one who unites practical and divine morality. He reverses all expectations about God, for us no less than for the Jews of his day. The unique, scandalous connection between the Kingdom, the meal and the sinner is visible in what he did and said. The Word of life and the Word of God are completely integrated in him.

Another Word which is equally shocking is also integrated for us in the Eucharist: the Word of the Cross. Paul describes this too as a scandal, the final reversal of expectation for the disciples. When we break bread in his name, we remember his body broken for us on the Cross and in the bread. This was not only for properly baptized

Christians but for all: he made no distinctions among those with whom he ate and those for whom he died.

An irony of church history has been the making of the crucifix into a barrier called the rood screen. Placed between sanctuary and people, priest and congregation, it separates them as surely as the priest in the Temple was separated from all others. The encouraging vision of the author of the Letter to the Hebrews is lost. For him, the Cross is not a barrier but the point of access, the edge of the abyss:

> Therefore, brethren, since we have confidence to enter the sanctuary by the blood of Jesus, by the new and living way which he opened for us through the curtain, that is, through his flesh, and since we have a great High Priest over the house of God, let us draw near with a true heart in full assurance of faith, with our hearts sprinkled clean from an evil conscience and our bodies washed with pure water (Heb. 10:19f).

This encouragement and confidence is as necessary for us as it was for those invited to table by Jesus. Zacchaeus gives a glimpse of the sheer incredulity with which sinners no less than Pharisees heard and accepted Jesus's invitation. For both, to eat with him meant publicly flouting the conventions.

What does this demand of us and our congregations? May we too find courage and confidence to enter one another's sanctuaries, undeterred by barriers of false righteousness. May we be united in the new and living way he has opened for us by sharing our common flesh, our bodiliness. His risen Body is our centre of purity. Certain of this, we can accept truthfully and joyously our common unworthiness, and refuse categorically to test one another's right to be there. For this new and open attitude is the verification of his presence among us. George Herbert has expressed it magnificently in his poem *Love*:

Love bade me welcome; yet my soul drew back,
   Guilty of dust and sin.
But quick-eyed Love, observing me grow slack
   From my first entrance in,
Drew nearer to me, sweetly questioning,
   'If I lacked anything.'

'A guest,' I answered, 'worthy to be here.'
   Love said, 'You shall be he.'
'I, the unkind, the ungrateful? Ah, my dear,
   I cannot look on Thee.'
Love took my hand, and smiling, did reply,
   'Who made the eyes but I?'

'Truth, Lord, but I have marred them: let my shame
   Go where it doth deserve.'
'And know you not,' says Love, 'who bore the blame?'
   'My dear, then I will serve.'
'You must sit down,' says Love, 'and taste my meat.'
   So I did sit and eat.

Herbert concentrates on the presence of Christ revealed in the indiscriminate love of the host. Christ is also present in the meal itself. Yet we have been discovering his presence among the sinners made welcome by the host. Thus, three truths emerge about the mystery of Christ's Body: he is present as Host, as Meal, as Guest, complete in each, no one devaluing the others. The first two are common topics in eucharistic discussion, but not the third. This understanding of the Eucharist identifies Jesus with those who hunger and thirst now, in our congregations as in the starving of the Third World.

This liberative vision is not new, but rather, a representation of the vision of Jesus outlined in the parables, and of Paul in his teaching on the celebration of the Lord's Supper. The first eucharistic assemblies we read of are those addressed by him. Jeremias dates Paul's letters to the Corinthians in *c.* 54 AD. In their celebrations of the Eucharist, the primitive church at Corinth experienced in a unique way the proximity, presence and society of its Lord. The body of Christ which we receive in the bread implied for Paul directly the body of Christ, in which we are bound together. We receive the body of Christ, and by receiving it we are, and show ourselves to be, the body of Christ.

Paul does not speak of eating the body and drinking the blood of Christ. Indeed, his formula does not express the simple equation, cup=blood. Nor does he say, in 1 Corinthians 10ff, that Christ is the miraculous drink which was given to Israel; but rather that he is the rock from which the water springs. Christ does not change himself into a sacramental substance but is the giver of the spiritual drink and spiritual food. Further, 1 Corinthians 10:16 speaks about the *breaking* of the bread and the *blessing* of the cup as sacramental acts, not about eating and drinking.

The conclusion drawn directly from Paul's eucharistic texts is that the 'body of Christ' received in the sacrament forms the 'mystical body of Christ' in the congregation. Discerning the body means understanding that the body of Christ given for us and received in the sacrament unites us in the 'body' of the congregation and makes us responsible for one another in love.

> If one member suffers, all suffer together; if one member is honoured, all rejoice together... You are the body of Christ and individually members of it (1 Cor. 12:26–7).

The numbers add up to something wonderful indeed: the presence of Christ in the congregation.

This means that the vision of the 'common' person, the woman or man who considers herself or himself 'nowt special', can be the catalyst for change in the church. Liberation theology relies on this. The powerless discover the power to change themselves, others and institutions when they discover that they themselves have been changed into the body of Christ through the free gift of the Spirit.

In the context of the eucharistic deprivation of other Christians, this liberative vision of Christ present in the congregation discerns him present also in other congregations, waiting for the invitation to table.

George Herbert describes this discovery and its consequences:

> Lord, I have invited all,
>   And I shall
> Still invite, still call to Thee:
> For it seems but just and right
>   In my sight,
> Where is all, there all should be.

CHAPTER 4

The Witness of the Holy Spirit

THE EARLY CHURCHES' understanding of Jesus' witness to God's indiscriminate love was not acquired once for all; it developed as they responded to the challenges of being Christian. One such crisis of growth provoked a major confrontation among the apostles and brethren. This was the mission to the Gentiles–or, as they are named in the parable, those outside the gates. For some time the apostolic communities remained strangely unaffected by their release from the letter of the Law. They continued to observe Jewish customs without being troubled by their full implications. They tried to steer a middle course between rigid exclusivism and Christ's all-inclusive commandment to love. But there came a point when they had to face up to the consequences of Jewish observance. Peter was the protagonist.

In the disconcerting fashion of the God of the Bible, a vision was given to someone outside the Jewish/Christian community which affected profoundly those within it. The pattern can be seen clearly at the time of the Babylonian exile, when 'the Lord stirred up the spirit of Cyrus King of Persia that he might build him a house at Jerusalem'. The result was the return of the Jews from exile, with the pagan Cyrus named as their Messiah, the Moses of their second Exodus (2 Chron. 36:22–3; Isa. 44:28ff).

The pattern is repeated in Peter's story told in Acts 10 and 11. Another pagan, a Roman centurion called Cornelius, is commanded by an angel to send for Peter. The next day Peter has a vision. He sees a great sheet let down from heaven which holds all kinds of animals, reptiles and birds. And there came a voice: 'Rise, Peter, kill and eat.' Peter refuses, because, 'I have never eaten anything that is common or unclean.' He is rebuked: what God has cleansed must not be called common. Offer and refusal, and presumably rebuke, take place three times. There are echoes here of his denial and confession of Christ.

What is Peter to make of this? His daring to refuse to obey the command, his perplexity at its nature, all point to unquestioning adherence by him and his brethren to the Jewish laws of dietary purity. But now he has been given a new commandment, to break these laws. While he is wondering what this can mean, the Spirit tells him that he has three guests and that he is to go with them. They are Cornelius's servants. Peter invites them in to stay the night, and presumably eats supper with them.

Next day he travels with them to Caesarea. He goes into Cornelius's house and talks with him and the others there. The step in understanding that he has taken in the power of the Spirit now becomes obvious. He has weighed up his vision and response and realized again the challenge of the Kingdom. He says: 'You yourselves know how unlawful it is for a Jew (!) to assoicate with or visit anyone of another nation; but *God has shown me that I should not call any man common or unclean*' (our italics). Cornelius tells him the story of the angel, and Peter responds in the same words Paul uses to the Romans: 'Truly I see that God has no favourites'. He goes on to give an account of Jesus, and describes himself as a witness who ate and drank with him after he rose from the dead. While he is still speaking, the Holy Spirit falls on all who are listening, pagans and circumcised alike. Then Peter commands that they all be baptized.

The reaction of the apostles and brethren in Judaea to the pre-emptive strike of the Holy Spirit is to blame Peter: 'Why did you go to uncircumcised men and eat with them?' From that initial decision all the rest had followed: the reception of the word of God; the gift of the Holy Spirit; the baptism of Gentiles. Peter had broken the letter of the Jewish Law. He defends himself against this charge by the unassailable assertion: 'The Spirit told me to go with them, *making no distinctions*' (our italics).

The lesson was heard and heeded. Those who had criticized him were silent, and then glorified God, saying: 'Then to the Gentiles also [the unclean, the outsiders, the unbaptized, the uncircumcised] God has granted repentance into life'. The catlyst for this expansion of the Kingdom was Peter's sharing of table companionship with the 'unclean'. On this depended whether or not the cup of the New Covenant was to be shared with all nations. Had the decision been otherwise, the primitive Christian community would have remained a Jewish sect, working only for the restoration of Israel.

The implications of this sequence of events are no less thought-provoking for present-day Christianity. There are some Christians who exclude other Christians from their churches unless they undergo another baptism. There are some who regard ecumenism as an optional extra, and some who ignore it altogether while pouring money into foreign missions to increase the numbers in their particular sect. And there are some who would share sacred meals with a reptile sooner than with those of a different denomination.

Bishop Richard Harries tells a story about these endemic divisions among Christians which should hurt us while we laugh at it. A Welshman was shipwrecked on a desert island. When he was rescued years later, he was asked why he had built himself two chapels, since he had been quite alone. The reply was that they were 'the chapel I go to, look you, and the chapel I don't go to!'

Sectarian Christians should re-read the story of Cyrus. Isaiah leaves us in no doubt about God's intentions in commissioning Cyrus to rebuild Jerusalem. God willed

that people from the rising of the sun and from the west
may know that there is no other God; that peoples from
all corners of the earth shall turn to God and be saved.
When the dispute about the admission of the Gentiles
erupts again, James sums up the implications of Peter's
vision by quoting this very passage from Isaiah (Acts
15:12–21). God had visited the Gentiles; had chosen them
to bear his name just as the 'outsiders' were compelled to
come in to the Great Banquet. It is a hard lesson for those
who consider themselves invited by right or rite, whether
Jew or Christian. The two stories in Acts show us how
slowly the lesson was learnt–and has to be continually re-
learnt.

Why is it so difficult? Given the fact of Christian
sectarianism as we endure it, what characteristics of the
Church foster and perpetuate a sectarian outlook? It is a
sombre fact that those Christian groups who have suffered
most from rejection, those who have been–and still are–
expelled from mainstream churches, tend to become in
turn savage persecutors of other groups. It seems incredible that seventeenth-century Puritan executioners of
Quaker women and men in Massachusetts could forget
their own persecution in England.

One possible reason for maintaining laws of exclusivity,
even at the cost of life, can be deduced from the story in
Acts. It echoes points made in preceding chapters of this
book. There is great security in law: the security of an
ordered existence in an ordered world. God is in heaven
and we all know our places on earth. These places are
marked out in various ways, and crossing the boundaries
leaves us vulnerable and uncertain. We are afraid of being
free to love. In the apostles' case, even after their public
affirmation at Pentecost and their first preaching, they
attempted to stay within the bounds of the Jewish Law.
They went up to the Temple, attended the synagogues
and observed the dietary laws. Although they spoke
'boldly', their behaviour was impeccably Jewish. Peter

appealed to his Jewish observance to justify his discriminatory behaviour. He relied on it to keep him pure. The effect of this reliance was that he and his fellow apostles re-built those walls which Jesus had torn down. They had forgotten his response to both the Samaritan and the Syro-Phoenician woman.

We are accustomed to think that the first Pentecost experience was totally decisive for the Church and to forget that it was one of a series. True, it drove the apostles physically out of the upper room and loosened the bonds on their tongues. But it took the pagan Pentecost of Cornelius and his brethren to drive them outside the spiritual walls of the Jewish Law. This experience broke the bounds of their table companionship. No longer could any food or person be barred from it on the grounds of uncleanness. God has created and called us all, and that alone is our security. The risen body of Jesus is our centre of purity, and as he told the disciples, unless we allow him to touch us in mutual service and make us clean, we have no fellowship with him, no place at his table (John 13:8).

This truth destroys the expectation that the 'good' deed makes us clean. It is a recurring temptation to attach values to our deeds and expect the price ticket to be endorsed by God. But the Jews recognize the fact that we cannot trust God to trade with our values. Rabbi Lionel Blue tells us a marvellous story of an Orthodox Rabbi dying and arriving in heaven. 'Who is in charge of the dietary laws here?' he asks. 'God,' he is told. 'In that case,' says the rabbi, 'I'll risk a piece of fruit.'

The fundamental law of creation, that God saw all that was made and it was good, must take precedence over man's assessment of what is good. The Law was intended as a guide to right living, not as a barricade against the rest of the world.

Using Cornelius as a test case, in the story in Acts, God protests against this misuse of the Law as a barrier. The apostles observed the dietary laws without questioning the fact that they had hardened into a code of restrictive practice against the Gentiles. The decisive step into Christianity meant discarding such practice. The God witnessed to by Jesus as he ate and drank with disciples and sinners has no truck with 'safe' distances between Christian and Jew, Christian and Gentile, Christian and Christian. As the Spirit forcefully reminded Peter, this God has *no* favourites.

The distance we place between ourselves and others is the measure of our own distance from God. When we cut ourselves off from others, we cut ourselves off from God's love. 'Where there is love there is God. Where there is no love God is absent.'* God's love and discrimination are mutually exclusive. When we reject each other, we are rejecting God. This is the nature of Christian blasphemy, to bear witness *against* the Holy Spirit that we are *not* all children of God. The worst blasphemy of all is to do this in God's Name; to call on the God of Jesus Christ to justify our hatred of those we reject. This is the Christian blasphemy of anti-semitism, made visible in the Holocaust. The psychoanalyst Thomas Szasz remarks sombrely:

> The moral aim of Christianity is to foster identification with Jesus as a model; its effect is often to inspire hatred for those who fail–because of their origins or beliefs–to display the proper reverence towards him.[1]

The spiritual barriers between Jew and Christian hardened into tangible walls in the ghettos and in Auschwitz. The concrete walls between Catholic and Protestant areas in Northern Ireland are a physical reminder of the spiritual barriers of hatred between two Christian communities.

---

*'Ubi caritas est, ibi Deus est. Ubi caritas non est, ibi Deus non est.'

'Security' forces patrol the barricades and keep them intact, whether with sermons or guns.

Perhaps because the communities are forced to face up to this tangible proof of their separation, some of the young people there find ways of working through these barriers. The Neighbourhood Open Workshop has created a street play called *Wall and Road*. Half the cast play Wall, and the other half play Road. Wall uses hexagonal blocks to obstruct, while Road has hexagonal paving slabs to open a way through. Two players, one from each side, act out a dialogue or play a match, and the audience votes on the winner, who then places a block or a slab in a strategic position. Each side is wonderfully persuasive and convincing, and the audience is swayed first one way and then the other. No one can predict at the start whether it will be victory for Wall or Road. It is a great relief to some of the adults when Road wins, but the more children there are in the audience, the more likely it is to be a victory for Wall.

This is hardly surprising. Children need security. So do adults, but they realize that they cannot have it at any cost. The vital step into maturity is the step outside the safeguards of the nursery into the great unknown. Beyond the wall 'Here be dragons'—but here also is adulthood.

When Peter and his brethren stepped outside the known security of Jewish Law they were not acting on their own intitiative. On the contrary: the Holy Spirit had driven them out, and Peter recognized this. He stressed the fact over and over again. The Spirit would not allow him to make distinctions. This was a hard truth for the apostles to accept, and their acceptance of it was gradual. We tend to think in terms of a once-for-all victory for the Spirit, but this was not the case. In Antioch the Holy Spirit chose Barnabas and Paul for the mission to Cyprus. On their return, they found that the controversy about Christians being circumcised had broken out again. They were sent to Jerusalem for a decision, where Peter repeated the previous arguments and conclusions. Once more they were endorsed by the brethren, and Barnabas and Paul brought their decision back to Antioch with the opening words: 'It has seemed good to the Holy Spirit and to us. . .' (Acts 15:28).

This process of learning to co-operate with the Spirit is evident throughout the Church's life from that day to this. Jesus' promise of the Spirit to his disciples is kept every time Christians move out from the security of Law to the insecurity of freedom to love. This freedom is the gift of the Spirit to the Church. Through this gift we recognize each other across the barriers of race, creed and culture as the children of God, created in God's image and sharing the bodiliness of Christ. Co-operation with the Spirit keeps this Kingdom vision clear. Its working principle is stated unambiguously by Paul: 'The Holy Spirit bears witness with our spirit that we are the children of God' (Rom. 8:16).

Bearing witness with the Spirit to the indiscriminate love of God is a continuous task. It becomes possible through what we shall call the eucharistic Pentecost. As the Eucharist has become the place where our separation is most obvious, it must again become the place where our witness to unity in the Spirit is most powerful. Lukas Vischer, in company with liturgical scholars of the Eastern and Western Churches, has said that the question of the Eucharistic *Epiclesis*, the calling on the Holy Spirit during the Eucharistic celebration, is of prime importance for ecumenical dialogue.[2] Liberative inter-church practices become possible when we deepen our understanding of this particular invocation of the Spirit.

Epiclesis is the name for the central prayer to the Holy Spirit in the Eucharist. It calls upon the Holy Spirit to be actively present, and in particular, to come upon the bread and wine and change them into the body and blood of Christ. There are many versions in many languages. One of the earliest, in Latin and Ethiopian, translates as follows:

> And we pray that you send your Holy Spirit upon the offering of your holy Church: gathering together in unity all those who partake of these holy mysteries so that they may be filled with the Holy Spirit unto the strengthening of the faith in truth.

A later one runs:

> We implore the merciful God to send forth his Holy Spirit upon the offering to make the bread the Body of Christ and the wine the Blood of Christ. For whatever the Holy Spirit touches is hallowed and changed (Cyril of Jerusalem, *c.* 385 AD).

The present-day *Epiclesis* in the Orthodox liturgy of the Eucharist belongs to the solemn central action, the Anaphora. It comes after the recitation and remembrance of the Last Supper narrative. The priest prays that God may send the Holy Spirit on us and on the gifts offered. He blesses the bread and says: 'Make this bread the precious Body of your Son'. Then the cup is blessed and prayed over. Blessing both together, he asks for them to be 'changed by your Holy Spirit'.

This unequivocal assertion of the vital role of the Holy Spirit in the consecration of the bread and wine is found in the Second Thanksgiving of the new Anglican Rite B, and in all those of Rite A. It is missing altogether from the Communion Service of the 1662 Prayer Book and the first official Eucharistic Prayer of the Roman Catholic Church. There is an ambiguous form of the invocation in the other three, but in all of them the invocation of the Spirit is placed before the Last Supper narrative. It introduces it instead of completing it.

In whatever form or wherever placed, these prayers are the crystallization of a process described by Paul as: 'the hallowing of the sacrifice of the Gentiles by the Holy Spirit' (Rom. 15:16). The Epistle to the Hebrews speaks of 'the blood of Christ, who through the eternal Spirit offered himself unblemished to God' (Heb. 9:14). These in turn reflect an understanding of the role of the Holy Spirit in the conception and life of Christ's body. Mary is told:

> The Holy Spirit will come upon you, and the power of the Most High will overshadow you; therefore the child to be born will be called holy, the Son of God (Luke 1:35).

Against this background the *Epiclesis* takes us into the mystery of the bodiliness of Christ, and the mystery of our own bodiliness. The Holy Spirit unites, hallows and transforms each of these, both in themselves and in relation to each other. The Spirit comes upon them and hallows them. Hallowing enables them to fulfil the purpose for which they are created. The Holy Spirit hallowed the body of Jesus that he might be called the Son of God. The Holy Spirit hallows our bodies that we might become the Body of Christ and be called the children of God. The third article of the Creed sums this up: in it we celebrate that the Body called Church is created and hallowed by the Holy Spirit in Baptism and Eucharist through the forgiveness of sins, and that the same Spirit that raised Jesus will raise our bodies also.

Such an understanding lies behind the petitions in the *Epiclesis* prayers. This invocation of the Spirit is the moment of real eucharistic power, the moment the community must reclaim. All ask for the Spirit; all are changed through union with the Spirit; all pray to be gathered in unity; all pray for the transformation of the bread and wine into the body and blood of Christ; all partake of it and of the one Spirit.

The communal nature of this petition for blessing on the community meal unites us also with the table companionship of Jesus' own community. One of the sources for the *Epiclesis* prayer is the Jewish meal blessing which asks for the Divine Presence to 'visit us on this day for blessing and save us on this day unto life'. If we take the *Epiclesis* seriously, we reclaim the unity of home and sanctuary, of the Word of God and the Word of Life. This removes distinctions in our minds and practices: all meals become sacred. The church on Sunday is not then treated as a sanitary district excluded from the pollution of ordinary life.

In an article on the church in Africa and contemporary social challenges, Kofi Asare Opoku points to the common perception of the church as a place where only 'decent' behaviour is allowed and only 'decent' problems can be aired:

> If the church is seen by its parishioners to be the place for only 'decent' problems, then it is not meeting the real needs of the people, social and spiritual. Such an understanding dichotomizes our lives; decent problems go to church on Sunday, and during the rest of the week, when we are engulfed in 'indecent' problems we take them to other places for solutions.[3]

Taking unity in the Holy Spirit seriously, we realize that it is the same Spirit who hallows the sacred Eucharist and the profane world, and by doing so unites them. Since this Spirit makes no distinction between 'clean' and 'unclean', neither must we. If we do, our spirit is not united with this Spirit in witness to the impartial love of God for all the created world.

Man-made barriers already exist within churches which isolate groups or individuals, making it impossible for us to bear witness together to the one Spirit. Common now to all mainstream Christian churches is the isolation of the cleric from the congregation. Observing the Orthodox Liturgy, it is clear that neither the recitation of the *Epiclesis* nor even a fanatical reverence for it are enough to destroy such isolating barriers. When did these barriers arise? How do they affect those on either side of them?

Edward Schillebeeckx gives a different picture of the possible relationship between community and leader. In the early church, he says, the link between them was so strong that to begin with it was impossible for the leader to be moved to another community save on compassionate grounds. Also, as a consequence of a canon of Chalcedon (451 AD), a minister who for any personal reason ceased to be the president of a community *ipso facto* returned to being a layman in the full sense of the word:

> In other words, according to this view it is not the case that someone who has the power bestowed by ordination may preside over the community and therefore also at the community's eucharist. The minister appointed by the community already receives, by virtue of his (*sic*) appointment, all the powers which are necessary for the leadership of a Christian community; he (*sic*) receives them from the Holy Spirit via the community.[4]

By the time of Charlemagne there was a tendency to separate the action of the priest during the ritual from that of the people. Ninth-century commentaries on the liturgy go on to stress that the liturgical action itself (including the invocation of the Spirit) belongs properly to the priest, rather than to the people of God as a whole acting as the body of Christ. There is a thirteenth-century manuscript which shows the completion of the process. It is entitled: *What the congregation is to do, think and say during the offering of Mass*. It is decorated with the familar picture of a cleric in Roman robes holding the Host up to heaven while the congregation is bent double in adoration and silence. By then, Schillebeeckx observes, the ecclesial dimension of the eucharist is reduced to the 'celebrating priest'.[5]

Such reduction led to the growth of private Masses in which the cleric assumed and performed the role of the laity in entirety. The cleric was indispensable, the laity were not. The 'invisible' Church justified its name and vanished.

This isolation of the cleric has been maintained by familiar (though largely unnoticed) structures of language and ritual. The kind of information communicated by the body language of the lone priest in the sanctuary, which Szasz calls 'protolanguage', is that the history of the world and of the church, the history of human effort and that of grace and salvation, are 'as two floors in the same building, with the upper floor inhabited by clergy alone'.[6]

The message of the protolanguage is reinforced by the spoken ritual. This makes the cleric articulate and keeps the laity silent. There is an assumption that the language of the eucharistic ritual and, in particular, that of the Institution narrative, has been placed outside time and history. It belongs to the upper floor inhabited only by ordained ministers and can be spoken only by them. This assumption in turn rests on an implicit distinction between earthly/secular/profane/material language and the sort that is heavenly/religious/sacred/spiritual. The first kind is used 'in the world' by the laity; the second belongs to eternity and the Church.

A practical demonstration of this thinking can be found just where it matters to us, in the question of the *Epiclesis*. In 1910 Maximilian of Saxony wrote an article bemoaning the division between the Roman and Orthodox churches.[7] He gave as one reason for its continuance the disregard of the Roman liturgy for the universality and centrality of the *Epiclesis* in the writings of the Fathers. This earned him a sharp rebuke from Pius X. The Pope rejected the appeal to the authority of the Fathers by appealing to the authority of Christ who, he said, intended the words he spoke at the Last Supper to be a liturgical consecration formula which cannot be changed.[8] We hardly need to comment on this. But nearer our time, a post-Vatican II Instruction on the Liturgy condemned the growing practice among the non-ordained of joining in with the priest at the conclusion of the consecratory prayer. What the cleric alone can do and say as Christ's representative is to be preserved intact.

The effect on the clergy of living behind these barricades

is incalculable. One assessment can be found in
Archbishop E. Milingo's reflections, in the article already
quoted, on the relationship between priest and people in
Africa. Talking of the problems of pastoral care, he
mentions the separation of pastor from parishioner which
makes it impossible for the latter to discuss his or her
problem with the pastor. He cannot remember, he says,
in the archdiocese of Lusaka, any parish priest who was
so trusted by his parishioners that they came to him with
their real problems. He offers as reasons the priest's
hesitant way of giving answers, the preaching of abso-
lutes, and the postponement of final decisions until a final
consultation. He asks:

> Is it strange then, that the people tend to believe that one can
> ask a priest only what he knows from his academic and
> theological studies and nothing beyond?[9]

With regard to the scandal of eucharistic discrimination,
it is practically impossible for the clergy as isolated
individuals to go against decisions made in the name of
the official Church they alone represent. Being under
orders to maintain 'good order', how can they disobey
orders to discriminate at the altar?

The effect on the laity individually is more obvious.
Made to feel dispensable, they dispense themselves from
attendance. Even in churches where private Masses are
unknown, the logic of dispensable congregations is working itself out inexorably. Congregations in the mainstream
churches dwindle. The community withers, and even-
tually dies.

So how can Leonardo Boff sound optimistic? He writes:

> We are living in privileged times. There is an upsurge of life
> in the Church that is revitalizing the entire body from head
> to toe. The Church has been placed on the road to renewal,
> which will surely result in a new manifestation of the Church

as institution. There are powerful and living forces, particularly at the grassroots, that are not sufficiently recognized by the traditional Church's present organization. The grassroots are asking for a new structure, a new ecclesial division of labour and of religious power. For this a new vision of the Church is necessary.[10]

What are these 'powerful and living forces, particularly at the grassroots, that are not sufficiently recognized by the traditional Church's present organisation'? In our second chapter we dealt with the mechanics of recognition and the barriers to it. The same barriers of law and ritual appear again in the situation of the cleric vis-à-vis the congregation. As with the recognition of Jesus himself, the proper recognition of the community as his Body can only happen through the power of the Spirit at work in both those who are unrecognized and those who must do the recognizing.

Boff asks for a new vision of the Church in order to bring about a new ecclesial division of labour and of religious power. We have been attempting to describe not a new ecclesial division, but rather a re-vision of Christ present in the eucharistic community. The power to live by this vision and to keep it clear is the gift of the Spirit. The *Epiclesis* is the place where that power is asked for and given, for it breaks down the barrier between priest and people, and unites them in the Body of Christ. This barrier must be destroyed first before the barriers between churches can be broken down.

The pattern of the pagan Pentecost in Acts has something else to tell us about the practical and living forces acclaimed by Boff. Cornelius was not just an outsider; he was the one unrecognized. Yet he forced Peter to recognize through the Holy Spirit the unity of humankind in creation.

In the mainstream churches today those who feel most keenly the isolating barriers of language, gender and law are the women. Their efforts to break these down force the churches to face the facts of discrimination at every level. Once they are faced, patterns of repression emerge, but correspondingly, patterns of liberation also. The discrimination against women, which denies them the right to preach or preside at Eucharists, underlines the dumbness imposed on the laity as a whole. Liberation means the power to speak on one's own behalf. It enables us to answer the call to a discipleship of equals.

The discrimination which denies women access to the sanctuary emphasizes the isolation there of the solitary man from the rest of the community. Liberation means the re-union of priest and people in the witness of the Body. Discrimination against women on the grounds of cultic pollution depends on discrimination by the 'righteous' against the 'sinner', by the 'clean' against the 'unclean', the basis of all barriers against full communion between churches. Liberation means recognizing the Eucharist as the forgiveness of sin through the presence of Christ in the power of the Holy Spirit.

Cornelius was told to invite Peter to his home. Peter came, and the rest is history. Women who cannot witness publicly to the indiscriminate love of God in church assemblies *can* do so in their homes. The same Spirit hallows both. Jesus' presence at the home in Cana for a marriage feast is part of the Kingdom vision of the Bible. The Kingdom of God will finally be celebrated as the joy of the marriage feast, the full communion of bodies (Matt. 22 and 25).

Such a feast is described by Isaiah. He speaks of the Lord preparing a banquet 'for all peoples' where death will be swallowed up for ever and all tears will be wiped away. The Lord will lay low the high fortified walls, and the pride of the people who built them. When he does, the walls cast down as dust will be trampled by 'the feet of the poor, the steps of the needy'. All the riff-raff will come in and be fed; the barriers will be broken; the way of the truly righteous will be opened up (Isa. 25:6 ff.). On that day, it will be the final victory over Wall for Road.

This victory has been made possible because Jesus' death tore apart the veil of the Temple. In doing so it tore down the wall between sacred and profane, between clean and unclean. When his body broke out of the tomb into Resurrection, it broke down the barrier between life and death. The Spirit invoked by our community in the *Epiclesis* is the Spirit of one who is risen, one who knows no bounds.

CHAPTER 5

The Witness of Faith

IT WAS NOW two days before the Passover and the Feast of Unleavened Bread. And the chief priests and the scribes were looking for a way to seize him and put him to death... Then Judas Iscariot, one of the twelve, went to the chief priests in order to hand him over to them... Now the betrayer had given them a sign, saying, The one I shall kiss is the man; seize him... And when he came, he [Judas] went up to him at once, and said, 'Rabbi!' And he kissed him. And they laid hands on him and seized him (Mark 14:1ff.).

In between these terrible events, Mark tells us, two things had happened; the anointing at Bethany and the celebration of the Passover. These major revelations of Jesus' power, and especially the power of his body, punctuate the narrative of betrayal. The body which will be given the deadly kiss of recognition by Judas is the same body anointed and kissed by the woman in recognition of its power to save. The body seized by the hands of the soldiers armed with swords and clubs is the body blessed and broken and given into the hands of the disciples.

Jesus commended the woman for what she did. Her act of extravagant love would become part of the gospel, to be proclaimed to the entire world in memory of her. She highlighted the value of Jesus' body as a source of blessing. Judas' decision to hand Jesus over to his enemies, made immediately after this event, showed that he shared their contempt for a body judged polluted and cursed by its association with sinners such as her.

The second event, the celebration of Passover, was the last of countless occasions at which Judas had seen and heard Jesus preside and teach at table. It was given particular solemnity by its setting within the environs of Jerusalem and the Temple, and by its emphasis on the sacredness of sharing bread. As usual, Judas had seen Jesus take and bless bread, and had then eaten it with him. But now he heard Jesus say that one of those eating with him would betray him. The dismayed incredulity with which the others heard this reminds us that, even apart from their own special and intimate relationship with Jesus, there was nothing so despicable in Jewish eyes as the betrayal of a companion—a fellow breadeater. Master and disciple, victim and betrayer had put their hands in the same dish. The sacred bread-bond of trust was broken. But woe to that disciple! It would have been better for him 'if he had not been born'.

This terrible denunciation by Jesus echoes through the centuries alongside his praise of the woman. She, who was cursed under the Law, touched Jesus with faith and was saved. Judas, who kissed him without faith, was cursed.

How could Judas do what he did? He had broken the bread-bond. His behaviour was consistent with the continuous misunderstanding of that bond shown by all the disciples throughout Jesus' ministry. Paul's words sound so simple to us now, and we repeat them so glibly. We forget all that it means to say: 'Because we share the one bread, we are the one body'. At this final meal, Jesus tried for the last time to teach his disciples its true meaning. He said over the blessed, broken and shared bread: 'Take, this is my body.' The bread they shared bound them together as his body. The bread that was broken was one with his body to be broken on the Cross. Both bonds of union were beyond their understanding, as they had failed to understand about the bread blessed, broken and shared with the multitudes in Galilee. 'They did not understand concerning the loaves, but their hearts were hardened' (Mark 6:52). Jesus berated them then: 'Do you not yet see or understand?.. And do you not remember concerning the loaves?' (Mark 8:16f.). Their incomprehension in Galilee foreshadowed their behaviour in Jerusalem. Even though Judas stands out through his treachery, the others too fall away. Jesus told them in the Garden of Olives: 'You will all be scandalized [*skandalisthesesthe*] in me' (Mark 14:27). Luke's account of this meal includes Jesus' warning addressed to Peter, and through him to them all: 'Simon, Simon, behold Satan demanded to have you (plural) that he might sift you like wheat, but I have prayed for you that your faith may not fail' (Luke 22:31f.). In spite of Peter's protestations of loyalty, Jesus tells him that he will in fact deny him.

Paul bears this out. Christ crucified, he says, is a stumbling block (*skandalon*) to the Jews. Discerning the Body in the bread and on the Cross depends ultimately on a particular kind of vision given through the Spirit. 'Now we have received not the spirit of the world but the Spirit of God, that we *might understand* the gifts bestowed on us by God' (1 Cor. 2:13f). This vision requires faith, which Jesus prayed that his disciples might have if they were not to deny him totally as Judas did. In the power of that vision, received when the Holy Spirit came upon them, they became witnesses in Jerusalem and Judaea and Samaria and to the ends of the earth that 'God has made him both Lord and Christ, this Jesus whom you crucified' (Acts 1:8, 2:36).

Discerning the Body in the bread and on the Cross requires faith from us. Discerning the body of Jesus for what it is—the gift of God—always has required faith. The woman understood who Jesus was and what he did, but Judas did not. Their understanding, or lack of it, accorded to their belief. They saw the same body, but they reacted to it in opposing ways and with exactly opposite effects.

The woman cursed under the Law touched Jesus with faith and was saved. Judas, one of the chosen, kissed him without faith and was cursed.

This pattern of reaction to Jesus through faith, followed by an effect on the believer, occurs throughout his public ministry. Typical of it is the story told in Matthew, Mark and Luke of the woman with a haemorrhage (and therefore permanently unclean). She heard what Jesus was doing and said to herself, 'If I touch him I shall be saved'. She managed to touch the hem of his garment and 'she knew in her body that she was healed... And Jesus, knowing power had gone out from him, turned in the crowd and said: "Who touched my garment?" And he continued looking about to see the woman who had done it. Then the woman, fearful and trembling, knowing what had happened to her, came and fell down before him and told him the whole truth. But he said to her: "Daughter, your faith has saved you. Go in peace"' (Mark 5:24ff. and parallels).

She knew in her body that by touching him she had drawn on the power and purity of Jesus' body. She knew her own uncleanness and unworthiness, and so she feared and trembled. The physicians at whose hands she had suffered, the laws which forbade her entry to the Temple and made her an object of pollution for twelve years had left her in no doubt about her status as diseased. For her to reach out and touch even the hem of Jesus' garment was an act of daring, liable to censure. Jesus' reaction, his search for 'the woman who had done it', reinforced her fear. His knowledge of her sex could only mean he also knew she was diseased. They both knew that he had been drawn into the circle of her uncleanness. The power and might of his body was linked to the weakness of hers in a relationship which saved and healed. He himself linked her faith to this mighty deed.

There is a passage in Luther which describes this encounter although it does not refer to it:

These three, Faith, Word and heart, become one. Faith is the bonding agent, Word and heart the opposites, but through Faith they become one Spirit, as man and woman are one flesh.[1]

The same witness of faith is clearly expressed in Luke's account of the anointing at Bethany. He tells us specifically that the woman is a sinner and that she kisses the feet of Jesus. At the close of the scene when her sins have been forgiven, Jesus says to this woman also, 'Your faith has saved you; go in peace'.

What emerges from all these encounters with the body of Jesus is his attitude to the man-made rules governing the right of access to him. According to these, the role of disciple bestowed a badge of worthiness to approach him, and the role of sinner meant automatic exclusion from his company. Judas had all the right credentials for unlimited access: he was a man, one of the chosen twelve, and as such he was an insider, part of the new hierarchy. The two women, on the other hand, started at a disadvantage because of their gender. Added to that, they were without status or worth, rank outsiders by life-style and physical condition, excluded from rite and by right.

Jesus' reactions to the individuals concerned invalidates any system of 'membership passes' to his presence. As the fences to the Royal Enclosure which men have built around him collapse, we find that the only condition for a saving encounter with his body is faith in the love which draws us to him.

This understanding of the faith bond with the body of Christ broken in the bread is part of Church tradition. Paul's teaching on discerning the body stresses the disposition of the receiver, which works for healing or damnation. A fourth-century East Syrian liturgy prays that the bread and the cup may become 'pardon for offenses and forgiveness of sins, a great hope in the resurrection of the dead and health of soul and body'. Ambrose teaches that 'whoever receives it [Eucharist] shall not die the death of a sinner, because this bread is the forgiveness of sins'. Augustine comments on the Bread of Life passage in John's Gospel: 'The Lord. . . called himself the bread of heaven exhorting us that we might believe in him. To believe in him; this is to eat living bread. Whoever believes, eats; invisibly he is nourished, because invisibly he is reborn.'

The necessity for belief can be observed in all the reactions to Jesus recorded in the Gospels. Early in his ministry when he went to Nazareth, his home town, he marvelled at the unbelief of those there, among his own kin and in his own household. Because of this unbelief he could do no mighty work among them. They looked at him and said: 'Is not this the carpenter's son? Don't we know his brothers and sisters? Can anything good come out of Nazareth?' Such scornful remarks revealed their inability to see the Lord of glory in such a body. Their disbelief roused them to outraged action, and they cast him out of the synagogue. In Luke's account of their rejection of Jesus they tried to throw him over a cliff (Luke 4:29).

In the sixth chapter of John's Gospel the necessity for faith in the person of Jesus and the need for faith in him as the bread of life are integrated. He says: 'I am the bread of life; he who comes to me shall not hunger, and he who believes in me shall never thirst. But I say to you that you have seen me and yet do not believe.' The response of the Jews is an amplification of that recorded by Luke: 'The Jews then murmured at him, because he said, "I am the bread which came down from heaven". They said: "Is not this Jesus, the son of Joseph, whose father and mother we know? How does he now say, I have come down from heaven?"' The narrative goes on with the teaching of Jesus about the necessity of eating his flesh and drinking his blood in order to live. It notes the murmuring of the disciples, and Jesus' knowledge of it. Then it brings together the themes of betrayal of his body and refusal to believe in the bread. 'For Jesus knew from the first who those were that did not believe, and who it was that should betray him' (John 6:35f.; 41f.; 60f.; 64f.).

Can this man Jesus, the son of Joseph, be the bread of life for the world? Those who listened to him and saw him were faced with this question. The disciples succeeded or failed in meeting this demand on their faith in varying degrees. The body of the carpenter's son was all they saw. The bread broken in his hands was still bread. According to tradition, bodies were clean or polluted; bread was sacred or ordinary. Those who worked with their hands or did not choose their company carefully had a very poor chance of being ritually clean. The bread of Presence in the Temple and the unleavened bread of Passover were sacred, but how could loaves coaxed from a boy who had followed the crowd be assessed? There could be nothing sacred about them. So how could ordinary loaves multiply—or how could they be multiplied in the hands of an ordinary man?

This personal dilemma of faith required the disciples to be convinced of something they could not see, and then to stake their lives on it. This requirement is not only characteristic of religious faith. At different stages of all our lives there is an element of risk when crucial decisions are made. To opt for one route rather than another requires acting in a half-blind way. We can never predict the outcome exactly. We cannot know from our own experience whether satisfaction or disaster will result. It is only after the event that we can say: 'It was (or was not) all for the best.'

This impossibility of knowing what still lies in the future keeps our actions free. We make decisions the consequences of which cannot be known fully. If we did know them, we would not be free, but would act for reward or punishment. The ability to take risks, and indeed the desire to do so, is part of a proper human response to life.

The making of decisions half-blind, and then acting on

them, is what is usually understood as 'acting in faith'. Reward or punishment assured beforehand would destroy our freedom and at the same time rob our faith of its peculiar qualities and abilities. This is true of all faiths, whether that of a child who puts a trusting hand into that of an adult in a dark place, or that of a disciple who responds to the terse command: 'Follow me!' without knowing where. There is an amusing but telling dialogue written by members of The Iona Community which makes the point well:

JESUS: Peter...?
PETER: Yes, Jesus...?
JESUS: Come with me.
PETER: Where are you going?
JESUS: I'm not telling you.
PETER: Do you not know?
JESUS: Oh yes, I've a fair idea.
PETER: Then...why won't you tell me?
JESUS: You might not like it.
PETER: Well, thanks for your consideration, Jesus.
      (*A pause*)
JESUS: Peter...?
PETER: Yes, Jesus...?
JESUS: Come with me.
PETER: Can I bring somebody else?
JESUS: Just bring yourself.
PETER: Will there only be two of us?
JESUS: Oh no, there'll be plenty of others.
PETER: Will I know some of them?...what about my cousin Alec...will he be there? and is there any chance of my sister coming if she still fancies you?..and what about my grannie? Oh, Jesus, I'd love to bring my grannie to meet you...Can I?
JESUS: Peter...just bring yourself.
PETER: But...but...you said there would be others.
JESUS: That's right.
PETER: Who are they?
JESUS: I'm not telling you.
PETER: Why not?
JESUS: You might not like them.

PETER: Aw, thanks a bunch, Jesus!

(*A pause*)

JESUS: Peter...?

PETER: Yes, Jesus???

JESUS: Come with me.

PETER: Jesus, I've got better things to do than go on a mystery tour. But I'll think about it. Just tell me what I'll need.

JESUS: Like what?

PETER: Like something to read in case I get bored...Like something to sing in case I get sad... Like a new pair of jeans in case there's a dance or a party.

JESUS: Peter, you'll not need anything. Just bring yourself. That's enough to contend with.

PETER: Jesus...do you want me to end up like you???

JESUS: Peter...I'm going...Are you coming with me?[2]

Even though Jesus said that our heavenly Father sees and rewards in secret, this did not provide Peter with an all-risks insurance policy. At the end of it all, the only certainty offered him was, 'When you are old, you will stretch our your hands, and another will gird you and carry you where you do not wish to go' (John 21:18).

The parable of the Last Judgment in Matthew's Gospel gives us some idea of how the Father rewards in secret. The good are amazed when commended for what they did without thought of reward. The Samaritan woman was repaid with the water of life for giving Jesus a drink, but according to both their traditions her action deserved censure, not praise. The Jewish parable recounted in Chapter 3 (page 45) in which God tells Moses of the gigantic treasure reserved in heaven for the undeserving, reinforces the difference between our scale of rewards and God's.

Juan Luis Segundo reaches an uncomfortable conclusion about the unknowability of results when we act in faith:

Seen from this strict point of view, the Christian faith of people who structure their lives in accordance with what they understand to be the supreme values conveyed by divine revelation in Jesus has nothing to do with the Christian 'faith' of those who receive a sacrament or take part in a Catholic procession *in order* to feel more secure before God or to obtain a 'grace' (our italics).[3]

In other words, if we do good deeds for a 'heavenly reward' rather than as a free response to the love of God, we are putting our faith in what they may achieve rather than in God's love.

So what kind of faith can we talk about or hope for when approaching the body of Christ? Already one characteristic of faith has emerged: its 'seeing darkly'. Nevertheless it is certainly 'seeing'. Its darkness is expressed famously: 'Faith is the assurance of things hoped for, the conviction of things not seen' (Heb. 11:1). But that leads on to further questions. What kinds of things? How do we know what to hope for?

Every time we use our freedom and choose to act in a certain way, we lose the possibilities offered by other choices. Faced with a complex realm of values beyond our own experience, we bring order to it by learning from others how to classify happenings and behaviour. We accept other people's valuations, their choices of some values rather than others beyond our capacity to explore. They become *referential witnesses* for us of the faith tradition into which we are born, helping us to articulate religious values in a largely unconscious but nevertheless effective way. In this way we learn to create our own scale of values.

We bring such a scale of values into play whenever we use the expression 'It's worth the trouble'. Originally the phrase 'for God's sake' must have had the same weight.

As we grow in faith we acquire habits of action. We learn the received traditions and how to conform to them. Then we behave automatically in traditional ways. But we must also learn to balance these against our own experience and make personal decisions based on our own judgment of the issues involved. We must decide for ourselves what really is of ultimate value.

The danger arises when the habit rules rather than the free decision. This is the behaviour which Jesus castigates as 'keeping the tradition of the elders rather than the commandments of God' (Mark 7:8).

The importance of referential witnesses to faith and the interaction between them and personal ultimate values can be seen in the life of Jesus. The author of the Letter to the Hebrews enumerates some of the witnesses for us. By faith, he says, Abraham obeyed when he was called to go out to a place he was to inherit, not knowing where it was. By faith Sarah conceived, even when she could see no possibility of the promised child in her aged body. He goes on through a 'great cloud of witness' until he comes to Jesus, 'the pioneer and perfecter of faith'.

The building up of his faith depended, as it does for us, on these witnesses. Although he lived in accordance with their scale of values, one particular value which he had learnt from his own life took precedence over all the rest. Segundo describes this as the Spirit of God operating with all its power.[4] This power, Jesus taught, is like the wind: it blows where it will and can be seen only in its effects. It is perceived through the events produced by its force. It drove Jesus out into the desert and on into his public ministry. It gave him power to forgive and to heal. It gives life to all creation without exception, and can be recognised wherever human beings recover their full potential.

This life-giving power makes no distinctions. It is the supreme value held by Jesus, and to reject it is therefore the supreme sin: this is blasphemy against the Holy Spirit. This stark contrast of values explains his saying that blasphemy against himself, ther Son of Man, will be forgiven, but not blasphemy against the Holy Spirit. Rejection of God's Holy Spirit is the absolute denial of

Jesus' absolute value. It is the other direction that a human being has the freedom to take.

How did this work out in Jesus' life? What was the effect of his faith, of his 'absolute value' on those around him?

For some, faith had hardened into routine observance. Their hearts and perceptions had hardened with it. Time and again Jesus warned them of this. In the Gospels lack of perception, hardness of heart and absence of faith are all synonymous with unbelief. The connection between faith and keeping rituals for their own sake is central to his teaching about the ritual food laws in Mark 7. Coming as it does between accounts of two occasions when he fed the multitudes, this teaching becomes the battleground for understanding the body of Jesus as the bread of life for the world.

The argument concentrates on what food can be counted pure or impure. Whenever people eat, says Jesus, it is not the keeping of a religious law which gives the meal value. Rather it is what is 'inside', what the heart bids a person do in the face of the needs of fellow human beings. He gives the devastating example of those who use a religious ritual in order to deprive their own parents. This empties the commandments, the word of God, of meaning. Tradition here reverses the fundamental scale of values in the Jewish scriptures. Jesus emphasizes this in a solemn formula which echoes the opening words of the daily recitation of Israel's Law: 'Hear me, all of you, and understand: nothing outside a man which goes into him can defile him, but the things which come out of a man defile him' (Mark 12:29f.; 7:14f.).

Mark tells us that after this, when he entered the house with his disciples, they asked him about this parable. Once again he asked them: 'Then are you also without understanding?' The battle for comprehension, that they might see the relationship between food, religious laws and human need, seemed no nearer a victory with them than with those 'who watched him, to see whether he would heal on a sabbath, that they might accuse him'. He looked at these with anger, grieved at their hardness of heart. The same hardness of heart afflicted the disciples. They could not see beyond the values which a religious law supposedly gives *in itself* to eating or any other action. They did not seem able to grasp that it is the intention of one human being towards another which, in Segundo's words, 'constitutes the one and only criterion, *however hazardous*, for determining the "Law", the will of God.'[5] To declare all foods clean shifted the criterion of worthiness for table companionship away from the security of keeping laws on to the dangerously uncertain level of love, trust, faith and loyalty.

This teaching is followed in both Mark and Matthew by a narrative which shows Jesus wrestling with the implications of his own statements. The greater detail in Matthew 15:21ff. makes clear how incredible this event must have seemed to the disciples. A pagan woman approached him and asked for healing for her devil-possessed daughter. She would have been even lower down the scale of religious observance than a Samaritan who at least would have known the Law of Moses. Jesus was ignoring her; the disciples begged him to send her away since she was a nuisance, crying after them.

When Jesus answered her it was merely to remind her that his mission was to the Jews alone. Undeterred, she came and knelt at his feet, beseeching him to help her. Jesus refused in the most insulting terms possible. It would not be right, he told her, to take bread from the children (Israel) and throw it to the dogs. By implication, she and her daughter were dogs with no claim to food set apart for human consumption.

But still she held her ground, reminding him of the oneness of the bread shared alike by the family seated round the table and the puppies scrounging scraps beneath it. Her tenacity is reminiscent of Jesus' parable of the man who begged bread from a friend at midnight, and was successful 'because of his importunity' (Luke 11:5ff.). Her persistence demonstrated her faith, and won the day for her. Jesus conceded her victory, the only time recorded in an argument with him. He praised her faith and healed her daughter. 'Then Jesus answered her: "O woman, great is your faith! Be it done to you as you desire." And her daughter was healed instantly' (Matt. 15:28).

This is the third time that we have mentioned Jesus praising a woman's faith. In the first two instances, those of the sinful woman who anointed him and the unclean woman who touched him, we looked at the pattern of reaction to Jesus through faith which has an effect on the believer. In this third instance, that of the Canaanite woman, she not only effected her daughter's cure but also affected Jesus' belief through her own. She did not belong to his faith tradition, yet forced him to overrule it.

Whenever people have tried to make 'outside' determinations of faith, says Segundo, within Christianity or not, they have in fact been devising a religious prescription that is 'human' in its origin, indulging in a religion of the 'lips' rather than the 'heart'.[6] Whether it is a piece of paper that one must have, or a certain religious observance, or even gender, any such external criterion is at best intended to represent an internal disposition. Jesus' encounter with the pagan woman shows him weighing his ultimate value of the indiscriminate power of the Holy Spirit witnessed to in her faith and courage against all such externals, and dismissing them in her favour. More than that, we see what lying witnesses they can be.

If we depend on legislating documents, for instance, as a guarantee of good faith, they become a substitute for the intention of the heart. In the long saga of events leading up to the excommunication of Archbishop Lefebvre, Peter Hebblethwaite reports, a conversation took place between Pope Paul VI and the French Catholic thinker, Jean Guitton. The latter asked the Pope what he would do if

Lefebvre repented. This raised the question of Lefebvre's sincerity. 'Sincerity is not guaranteed,' Paul VI remarked, 'by a form of words or a statement which, for someone as inconsistent as Mgr Lefebvre, will be followed tomorrow by a contrary statement.'[7]

The New Testament discussion of religious laws about food exposes the anomaly of present laws of discrimination in eucharistic table companionship. Jesus's own preaching and practice declared unequivocally that the sacredness of bread does not depend on a religious law which judges either the bread or the eater 'pure', but on the sensitivity and faith of the human heart which receives it. The sacredness of the bread we share in the Eucharist is no different from the sacredness of the bread we share on our tables. All bread is 'clean' when it is shared with hearts which try to harbour no evil thoughts, fornication, theft, murder, or, we may add, discrimination. Jesus knew what was in Judas' heart when he pronounced his terrible judgment on him. The other disciples could see no difference between his table companionship and their own. There is no record of their reaction to Jesus' exchange with the Syro-Phoenician woman, but we have enough evidence from other occasions to guess what it might have been. Peter's sanctimonious response to the suggestion that he ought to eat with Cornelius is sufficient.

Laws of eucharistic discrimination which we endure today try to define what is sacred bread and who is worthy to touch it. At this point the laws about the sacredness or otherwise of bodies become relevant. What body was more sacred than that of Jesus? Who had acces to it? What were the visible effects on those who touched him?

It is perhaps the last question which shows us a way forward. If we say that those who touched him with faith were saved or healed, and those who touched him without faith were damned, then it seems we have only substituted an impossible criterion for an unacceptable one. Blue, white and velvet collars can at least be counted. Baptismal and Confirmation certificates can at least be read. Ecumenical statements can be pondered and checked for mistakes. How can we rely on the sacredness of a bread-bond which does not depend on the precepts or practice of men but on what is in the heart, the place of unseen desires?

This is not a new problem. It appears in the New Testament immediately after the death of Jesus. In the Gospels the problem is cloaked by the fact that Jesus is seen in his Risen Body. 'Because you have seen me you have believed,' Jesus says to Thomas. This seeing serves as a focus for the sacredness of eating and drinking together. It is extraordinary how many accounts of different meals there are in the resurrection narratives, some hosted and prepared by Jesus and some not. One in particular, the meal with the disciples at Emmaus, is noteworthy for the fact that it was not the teaching of Jesus (his interpretation of the Scriptures) which convinced the disciples of his presence among them, but seeing him take the ordinary bread sold in a wayside inn and breaking it with them.

Paul and James had the same problem as us of recognizing and defining faith in the body, and solved it in ways which are no less valid today than then. They built on the startling injunction of Jesus that, when we come to offer our gift at the altar and there remember that our brother has anything against us, we are to leave the gift before the altar, go and be reconciled with our brother and then come and offer the gift (Matt. 5:23). The sequence of action is important. The onus is on us to seek reconciliation, even though it is another who bears the grudge against us. How long it takes to be reconciled—hours, days or years—is not mentioned. It takes as long as it takes. There is no statute of limitations to ease our consciences. There our gift must stay until we have restored harmony.

This is in line with prophetic tirades against religious observance which offers sacrifices and prayers in the Temple while the widow and orphan are neglected. Isaiah and Amos were uncompromising in their rejection of this behaviour. Such external acts of faith stink in God's nostrils and are an abomination in God's eyes. Those who perform them honour God with their lips while their hearts are far from him.

These injunctions give Paul and James the guidelines they need to establish a faith criterion for approaching the body of Jesus present in the one bread. Our behaviour towards the other members of that body acts as monitor on our faith. Faith cannot be assessed as such, but its effects on our behaviour towards others can be gauged. In the practice of table companionship the harmony and reconciliation between the companions determines the Eucharist. If there is no care for one another, then the Lord's Supper is not celebrated. The bread is broken for judgment and not for blessing.

Paul concentrates on some evil practices, which have been adopted by the Church at Corinth, that vitiate the sacredness of eating the Lord's Supper. Indeed, they ensure that it is *not* the Lord's Supper, even though bread is broken and shared and wine drunk in remembrance. There are divisions among the companions; those who have food go ahead and eat it; some are drunk; others have neither food nor drink and are humiliated by those who have. With such behaviour the Lord's Supper is not celebrated, even though formal prescriptions are followed. Instead, the body and blood of the Lord are profaned. Those who eat and drink are judged, because they have not discerned the one body into which we are all baptized by the one Spirit. Paul exhorts them: 'So, my brethren, when you come together to eat, wait for one another, lest you come together to be condemned' (1 Cor. 12:13; cf. 11:17ff.).

It seems hard to credit that what appears as no more than good manners decides the nature of our Eucharists. But courtesy and charity live together. The one is the public face of the other. Formal courtesies can appear mere formalities, but they are much more. Jesus noticed that Simon had denied him the formal kiss of welcome, and understood this to be more than forgetfulness. Archbishop Tutu tells of his mother's first meeting with Bishop Huddleston, which made an indelible impression on her because he raised his hat and greeted her with the same courtesy that he would have given to a white woman.

We are back with the habitual nature of our behaviour, which is largely unconscious. We adopt the manners and customs of those we have as referential witnesses. But courtesy must always be kept from mere formality by making it a true expression of our values. This is no less the case whether we share a 'sacred' meal, dine at the Ritz, or give bread to a beggar at the back door.

James focusses on another set of behaviour patterns at formal worship, and connects them explicitly with faith. 'My brothers,' he says, 'do not try to combine faith in Jesus Christ with the making of distinctions between classes of people' (2:1).

This command rings very hollow in our ears when we recall how often 'faith' is used to do just that. Not long after the time of James, relatively speaking, the catechumens were segregated from the 'faithful'. The march towards orthodoxy and separation was on.

James goes on to give an example from 'church' practice which at first glance has little to do with faith in Jesus Christ. 'Now suppose a man comes into your synagogue [!], beautifully dressed and with a gold ring on, and at the same time a poor man comes in, in shabby clothes, and you take notice of the well-dressed man, and say, "Come this way to the best seat"; then you tell the poor man,

"Stand over here" or "You can sit on the floor by my foot-rest", haven't you made distinctions among yourselves, and become corrupt judges?' (2:2ff.).

The experience of the Lutheran student in America mentioned in Chapter 2 (pp. 40–41) immediately comes to mind when reading this today. Patterns of behaviour are just that, patterns which repeat from one generation to another. Placed in contrast to the faith patterns of Jesus, they must be checked by each generation to see how far they have deviated from his norm. James found it necessary in his lifetime, and it is no less essential in ours.

Then, as now, Jesus' norm regulates a scale of values which does not reject the poor. But these are precisely the ones pushed to one side by church protocol, because this operates with a scale of values which judges by externals. James reminds his readers what it means to fulfil the law, the royal law of Scripture. This is to love your neighbour as yourself. 'But as soon as you make distinctions between classes of people you are committing sin and are condemned by the law' (James 2:8).

Jesus did not retrace Abraham's journey to Ur or Jacob's crossing of the Jabbok. He lived out his faith in his own time by a series of decisions that took him ultimately to Jerusalem and death. The final test of his faith took place on the Cross, when the terrible consequences of his decisions included the experience of being abandoned by the Father. The Spirit who raised him from death was the same Spirit whose power to fulfil human potential, including his own, had been the supreme value of his life. His faith was vindicated in Resurrection.

With him as our referential witness, we too are to live out our faith in the time and place in which we live. Paul and James have shown us how to monitor this hazardous criterion when we come together to celebrate the Eucharist. Faith in the body is shown by mutual care, by a lack of divisions among us and by a refusal to make distinctions other than towards the poor. Our decisions about

one another's status, about who has access to the body of
our companionship and who has not, are reliable indica-
tors of the scale of values with which we operate.

If we take our New Testament witnesses seriously, we
find that over a long period of time the decisions that have
been made about church order operate more and more
with a scale of values alien to them. The preceding
chapters give many examples. In regard to the correlation
between our behaviour towards fellow Christians and the
validity of our eucharistic celebrations, the alienation
appears complete.

A prime example of this is the acceptance of the
'ecumenical' principle that until individual churches have
agreed on the nature of ministry to *their* satisfaction, each
one must break bread *alone*. This turns the New Testament
witness to faith in the body upside down. It is worth
repeating what Jesus said: 'So if you are offering your gift
at the altar, and there remember that your brother has
something against you, leave your gift there before the
altar and go; first be reconciled to your brother, and then
come and offer your gift' (Matt. 5:23–4). In obedience to
this injunction all eucharistic celebrations should be
suspended until the churches are reconciled.

This time could be used to repent of the divisions, and
to prepare for a common act of reconciliation–common as
to time, diverse as to expression (each church working out
its own). The Stuttgart Confession of the German churches about the role of Christianity in the Holocaust is a
model of the sort of declaration of guilt and repentance
necessary. The willingness of individual churches to
participate would indicate their willingness to accept other
churches as equal companions in the one bread we all
share. The lopsidedness of present practice emphasises
the culpable pride of churches which 'go it alone' on the
assumption that they alone are the Church.

Instead of showing faith in one another through mutual
building up of the body, above all in looking after the

needs of those who hunger and thirst for the bread of life, we appear to place our faith in the 'lips', in statements and definitions that can never, as Paul IV confirmed, guarantee the 'heart'. We are back with the denunciation by Jesus of those who use 'traditions' in order to deprive their own flesh and blood of the necessities for life.

This leads on to the relationship between the body of the faithful, as it is usually called, and the body of the accredited minister. The distinction made between them in some churches today highlights a consequence of the decision to concentrate on statements about ministry in order to reach full communion between the churches. It supposes that the faith of the eucharistic community centres on faith in its ministers, that is, on the validity of their ordination. The certainty denied to the disciples is guaranteed to a church congregation which insists that its minister is 'essentially' different from all the other members of that body. The ordained hand is sacred, in distinction from all others.

Any hope that this might be a caricature of church faith disappears as soon as one reflects on the passions aroused and schisms endured or promised whenever ordination is debated in a way which threatens such a distinction. Whether the focus is on gender or the 'essential' difference, the reactions speak for themselves. They witness to a faith centred on certainty. But that is not the faith in his body that Jesus asked for.

This certainty is not simply centred on ordained ministry. It has been inextricably bound to it since the time of Ignatius of Antioch. Whatever he meant when he wrote to the churches on his way to Rome and martyrdom *c.* 114 AD, he is quoted time and again in Vatican documents to establish the principle of apostolic succession. This teaches that the bishops of one particular church, in distinction from all others, are the vital link between the work of Christ and their congregations. Not only that, they are the vital link between them and the Holy Spirit.

The Vatican II document *Lumen Gentium* is quite clear on this. The bishop presiding at the Eucharist, 'which he offers or causes to be offered', is the 'steward of the grace of the supreme priesthood'. With(out) his presence, or those who represent him, 'the mystery of the Lord's Supper is (not) celebrated.' The reason given is that the faithful are united in the presence of Christ only when they are 'united with their pastors'.[8]

The kind of certainty claimed in such statements brings us back to the theme of security and its ever-present attractions. In this instance, such teaching about ordained ministry necessarily creates impregnable barriers against all those who live outside them. But what a vision of security for those within! It seems to make it possible for them to break the bread-bond with other Christians, either by refusing them bread from their own altar, or rejecting it from other Christian altars.

It is well to be clear that such teaching necessarily precludes a documentary unity which takes honest account of the diversity of gifts bestowed by the same Spirit on different churches. It accords ill with Paul's exhortation to the Romans of his time not to think of themselves more highly than they ought, 'but to think with sober judgment, each according to the measure of faith which God has assigned him' (Rom. 12:3). This acceptance of the limitations of one's own 'measure' of faith is not a recipe for division but for diversity in unity. 'For as in one body we have many members, and all the members do not have the same function, so we, though many, are one body in Christ, and individually members one of another' (Rom. 12:4–5). The basis for this unity of the body is the recognition that all have differing gifts according to the grace given, according to the measure of faith assigned. No monopolies are allowed.

Attempts to live with monopolies lead to exhortations to the churches to 'co-operate on every level', with honourable mention given to the bottom level, the ladies

who do the floors and flowers. But at that level there is
no problem. The hands which scrub and draw water claim
no special status for themselves. The scandal is that this
is used as an argument against their handling the body of
Christ for others.

An unnamed poet has expressed this thought in the
following:

> Did the woman say, as she held him for the first time,
> in the dark of the stable,
> after the pain, the bleeding and the crying,
> This is my body, this is my blood.
>
> Did the woman say, as she held him for the last time,
> in the dark of the garden,
> afte the pain, the bleeding and the dying,
> This is my body, this is my blood.
>
> Well that she said it for him then,
> for dried old men,
> brocaded robes belying barrenness,
> ordain that she not say it for him now.

What body was more sacred than that of Jesus? Who
had acces to it? What barriers did he place between
himself and those who wanted to touch him? It is part of
the mystery of his faith that his belief in the potential of
every human being through the power of the Spirit forced
him, as we saw with the Syro-Phoenician woman, to deny
access to no one. This belief led him to give unlimited
access to Judas. He could not deny it without denying the
power of the Spirit even in him. To do so would be the
supreme unpardonable sin. And even though Judas
kissed him without faith, and was denounced by Jesus,
we are told that he repented. And so there is a baroque
church in Southern Germany which includes Judas among
the canonized apostles.

The poet Sydney Carter sums up the connection
between the faith of the Church and the faith of Jesus. The

function of the Church, he says, is not to rush around getting pagans, Jews, Buddhists or anyone to sign a legal document saying, 'I believe there was a man called Jesus, and he was the Son of God'. The function of the Church is to embody the hope, the danger, the beauty and the possibility held out by Jesus.[9]

Notes

INTRODUCTION (pages 1–13)

1. Jürgen Moltmann, *The Church in the Power of the Spirit* (London: S.C.M. Press, 1977), p.17.

2. James Baxter, *Jerusalem Daybook* (Wellington: Price Milburn & Co. Ltd, 1971), p.8.

3. See R.A. Alves, *Protestantism and Repression* (London: S.C.M. Press, 1985).

4. James Baxter, *Autumn Testament* (Wellington: Price Milburn, 1972), p.35.

5. José Míguez Bonino, *Unity between Hope and History* (Barnsley, South Yorkshire: One for Christian Renewal, No. 2, 1983).

6. See Edward Schillebeeckx, *Ministry* (London: S.C.M. Press, 1981), p. 39.

7. Bonino, ibid.

8. See Frank Muscat, 'A Chaplain's Dilemma', *The Tablet*, 22 October 1988, p. 1228.

9. Bonino, ibid.

10. See *The Tablet*, 21 January 1989, p. 68. Mrs J. O'Rourke wrote of her sixteen-year-old daughter's explanation of why she and her brothers refused to have anything to do with the Church:

Priests,
said my daughter,
treat the church like a cake,
a marvellous cake.
Made by a master baker.
And unique. Unrepeatable.
How wonderful, they say,

101

examine the perfection.
Enough for everyone,
if only we dare share it.

Priests,
said my daughter,
speak about it constantly,
discuss its origins,
ingredients, embellishments.
They sigh over the icing cracks,
regret decorations
lost or crumbling.
Irreplaceable, they say.

Priests,
said my daughter,
are great preservers,
keepers, guardians,
curators reading recipes
among their footnotes.
And yet the master stands,
apron and hands floured white,
waiting
with fresh bread for the poor.

CHAPTER 1 (pages 15–24)

1. Sallie McFague, *Models of God: Theology for an Ecological, Nuclear Age* (London: S.C.M. Press, 1987), p.52.

2. See Joachim Jeremias *Jerusalem in the Time of Jesus* (London: S.C.M. Press, 1969): 'Samaritans were considered from the cradle [i.e. always] as impure in a very high degree, and as causing impurity. This refers to the rule that Samaritan women were considered to be "as menstruants from the cradle", and their husbands as perpetually unclean for that reason.... Because of this any place where a Samaritan lay was levitically unclean, and likewise any food or drink which had touched the place. Thus a traveller through Samaritan territory who accepted food or drink from them could never know if it was clean or not. By the same rule, moreover, the spittle of a

Samaritan woman was unclean; and if one such woman stayed in a town, all spittle there was unclean.' p. 356f.

3. C.K. Barrett, *The Gospel according to John* (London: S.P.C.K., 1955), p. 191.

4. Juan Luis Segundo, *The Historical Jesus of the Synoptics*, (London: Sheed and Ward, 1985), p. 131f.

5. *Christ and the Samaritan Woman*, Icon from last quarter of fifteenth century, Kanellopoulos Museum, Athens.

6. See Jeremias, op. cit., p. 375, n. 83.

CHAPTER 2 (pages 25–43)

1. Brendan O'Regan, 'The Third Way: Through the Wandering Rocks', *The Crane Bag*, Dublin, Vol. 9, No. 2, 1985, p.160.

2. John Coventry, 'Theology of Ministry', *New Blackfriars*, Oxford, Vol. 68, No. 810, 1985, p.484.

3. Juan Luis Segundo, *Theology and the Church* (London: Geoffrey Chapman, 1985), p. 110f.

4. Brendan O'Regan, op. cit.

5. Juan Luis Segundo, *The Liberation of Theology* (Dublin: Gill and Macmillan, 1977), p. 86.

6. Juan Luis Segundo, *The Historical Jesus of the Synoptics*, p. 39.

7. Joachim Jeremias, *The Parables of Jesus* (London: S.C.M. Press, 1963), p. 126f.

8. Joachim Jeremias, *The Eucharistic Words of Jesus* (London: S.C.M. Press, 1966), p.66.

9. Juan Luis Segundo, *Theology and the Church*, p. 84.

10. George Johnston, *The Spirit-Paraclete in the Gospel of John* (Cambridge: University Press, 1970), p. 47.

11. Columba Stewart, 'Mixed Reception', *The Tablet*, 6 June 1987, p. 603f.

12. Joachim Jeremias, *The Eucharistic Words of Jesus*, p. 204.

13. Juan Luis Segundo, *Theology and the Church*, p. 59.

CHAPTER 3 (pages 44–58)

1. See John Dominic Crossan, *Finding is the First Act* (Philadelphia: Fortress Press, 1979), p. 53f.

2. Kofi Asare Opoku, 'The Church in Africa and Contemporary Sociological Challenges', *The Ecumenical Review*, Vol. 40, No. 2, April 1988, p. 253.

3. ibid.

4. Juan Luis Segundo, *The Humanist Christology of Paul* (London: Sheed and Ward, 1986), p. 124.

5. Fritjof Capra, *The Turning Point* (London: Fontana, 1983), p. 285.

6. E.P. Sanders, *Paul and Palestinian Judaism* (London: S.C.M. Press, 1977), p. 455.

This does not legitimize the exclusion of polygamists from the Lord's Supper, since fornication (a union between man and woman *without* responsibility for the woman or her children) cannot be compared to legal union between a man and his wives which *accepts* responsibility for women and children.

7. J.D. Crossan, *The Dark Interval* (Illinois, Argus Communications, 1975), p. 125f.

CHAPTER 4 (pages 59–75)

1. Thomas Szasz, *The Manufacture of Madness* (New York: Harper and Row, 1970), p. 262.

2. Lukas Vischer, 'The Epiclesis: Sign of Unity and Renewal', *Studia Liturgica 6* (1969), 30–39.

3. Kofi Asare Opoku. 'The Church in Africa and Contemporary Sociological Challenges', *The Ecumenical Review*, Vol. 40, No. 2. April 1988, p. 250.

4. Edward Schillebeeckx, *Ministry* (London: S.C.M. Press, 1981), p. 4.

5. ibid. p. 54.

6. Juan Luis Segundo, *Theology and the Church*, p. 84.

7. Maximilian of Saxony, 'Pensées sur la question de l'union des Eglises', *Roma e l'Orient 1* (1910), 25.

8. See John H. McKenna, *Eucharist and Holy Spirit* (Great Wakering: Mayhew-McCrimmon, 1975), p. 86.

9. Opoku, op. cit., p. 250.

10. Leonardo Boff,. *Church: Charism and Power* (New York: Crossroad and London: S.C.M. Press, 1985), p. ix.

CHAPTER 5 (pages 76–99)

1. Martin Luther, *Kritische Gesamtausgabe* (Weimar: 1883), 57, 156.

2. John Bell & Graham Maule, *Seven Dialogues* (Glasgow: Wild Goose Publications, 1987), p. 3ff.

3. Juan Luis Segundo, *Faith and Ideologies* (London: Sheed & Ward, 1984), p. 39.

4. ibid, p. 48.

5. ibid. p. 44.

6. ibid. p. 45.

7. Peter Hebblethwaite, 'The Road to Schism', *The Tablet*, 3 September 1988, p. 1009.

8. Walter Abbott, ed., *The Documents of Vatican II* (London: Geoffrey Chapman, 1966), p. 50.

9. Sydney Carter, *Dance in the Dark* (London: Fount, 1980), p. 27.

Suggestions for Further Reading

Belo, Fernando. *A Materialist Reading of the Gospel of Mark*. (Maryknoll, NY: Orbis Books, 1981).

Benko, Stephen. *The Meaning of Sanctorum Communio*. (Illinois: Allenson Inc., 1964).

Dodd, C.H. *The Parables of the Kingdom*. (Glasgow: Fontana, 1961).

Dunn, James D.G. *Baptism in the Holy Spirit*. (London: S.C.M. Press, 1970).

Dunn, James D.G. *Jesus and the Spirit*. (London: S.C.M. Press, 1975).

Fiorenza, Elizabeth. *In Memory of Her*. (London: S.C.M. Press, 1983).

Kermode, Frank. *The Genesis of Secrecy*. (Cambridge, Mass: Harvard University Press, 1979).

Macy, Gary. *Theologies of the Eucharist*. (Oxford: Clarendon Press, 1984).

Perrin, Norman. *Jesus and the Language of the Kingdom*. (London: S.C.M. Press, 1976).

Williams, J.G. *Those Who Ponder Proverbs*. (Sheffield: Almond Press, 1981).

Williams, J.G. *Women Recounted*. (Sheffield: Almond Press, 1982).

Macy, Gary. *Theologies of the Eucharist*. (Oxford: Clarendon Press, 1984).

Perrin, Norman. *Jesus and the Language of the Kingdom*. (London: S.C.M. Press, 1976).

Williams, J.G. *Those Who Ponder Proverbs,*. (Sheffield: Almond Press, 1981).

Williams, J.G. *Women Recounted.* (Sheffield: Almond Press, 1982).